The All Color World of
CARS

The All Color World of
CARS

Phil Drackett

octopus

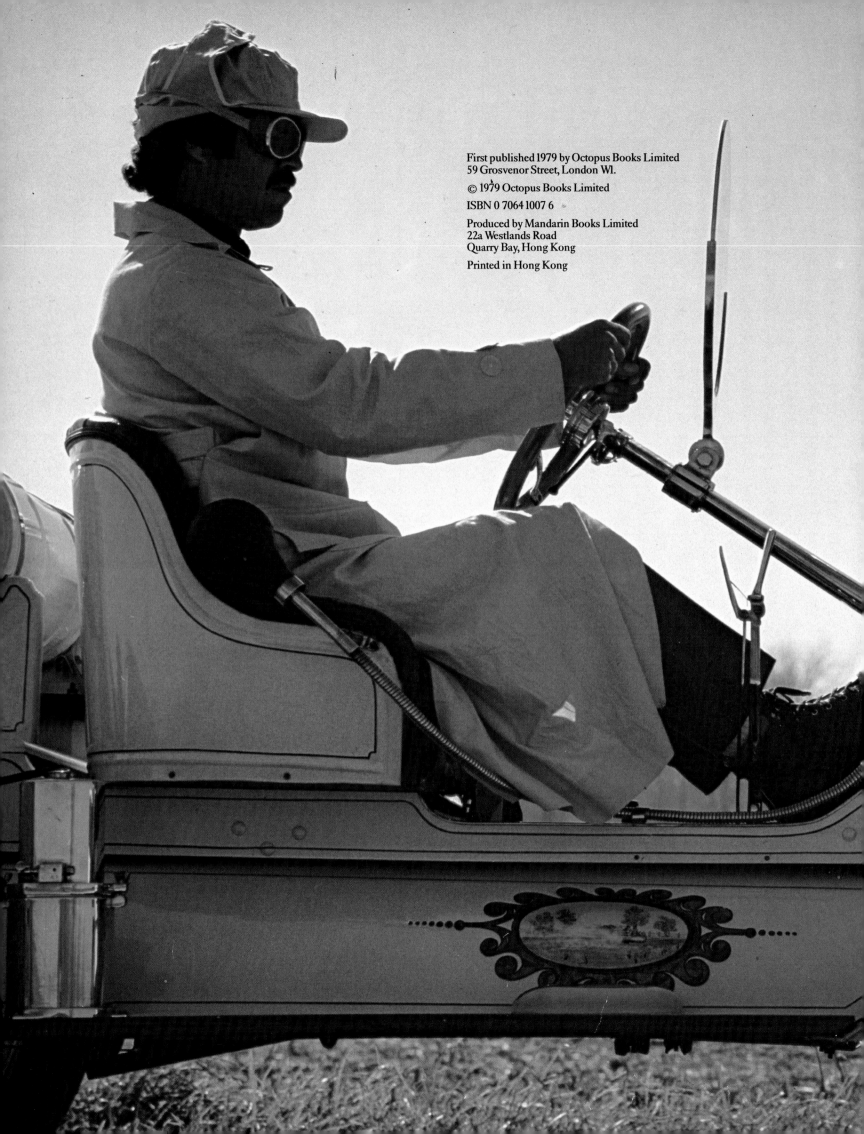

First published 1979 by Octopus Books Limited
59 Grosvenor Street, London Wl.

© 1979 Octopus Books Limited

ISBN 0 7064 1007 6

Produced by Mandarin Books Limited
22a Westlands Road
Quarry Bay, Hong Kong

Printed in Hong Kong

Contents

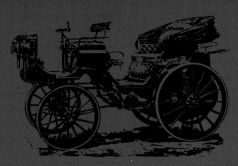

Who Invented the Car?

On a house in Malchin in Austria is a plaque which reads 'Birthplace of Siegfried Marcus, Inventor of the Automobile, born September 18th, 1831'. But was Marcus the inventor of the motor car? The arguments have raged for many a year and rival claims have come from all over the world.

To try and assess the situation it is necessary to decide what constitutes a motor car. Certainly, the well-used term 'horseless carriage' is not enough. If it were, then the anonymous gentleman who designed a horseless carriage, propelled by wind, in 1475, was the true inventor of the car. Following him came the Emperor Maximilian who, in 1520, invented a lever-propelled horseless carriage. This relied upon men walking beside the vehicle to pull the levers, which rather defeated the object of the exercise, men being rather slower than horses. And between 1657–67 a Jesuit priest, Father Ferdinand Verbiest, is said to have built some sort of self-propelled vehicle in China.

The first truly successful horseless carriages were, in fact, steam-driven. Thomas Newcomen created the steam engine as early as 1712 and it was greatly improved by another British engineer, James Watt. But it was the Frenchman, Nicholas Joseph Cugnot, who first adapted the steam engine to propel a vehicle. He is said to have built a model steam carriage in 1763, however, be that as it may, in 1769 he produced the first of his two full-size steam carriages and it is to him that most experts give credit for the first mechanical road vehicle in the world.

Cugnot was a French artillery officer and his vehicle was intended to be a self-propelled gun carriage. Unfortunately, the weight of the boiler at one end was so great that if the gun were taken off, the carriage toppled over. In any event, it was unstable and difficult to steer. The first carriage ran into a wall and

the second, built in 1770, overturned on a Paris street-corner. It is still preserved in Paris and a large-scale model is kept in the Royal Automobile Club, London.

Cugnot's efforts were followed by more practical developments and the 19th century was the heyday of steam-propelled vehicles, both on the roads and on rail. In England Richard Trevithick, William Murdock, Sir Goldsworthy Gurney, William Symington, Thomas Rickett and Robert Fourness, among others, played leading roles in developing these vehicles. In Czechoslovakia, Joseph Bozeck built and drove a steam car in 1815. In France, Amedee Bollée Senior produced a steam omnibus in 1873. This was remarkable because the front wheels were independently sprung and pivoted individually on separate stub-axles, all foreshadowing the modern car.

The Comte de Dion (1884) and Leon Serpollet (1887) were two other Frenchmen who built highly successful steam road vehicles, and in the United States of America, the Stanley and White steam cars – the first prototypes of which appeared in the 1890s and were very popular for many years. Eventually, however, the steam car faded into obscurity.

This brings us back to the definition of a motor car. What most of us mean by motor car (or automobile) is a vehicle driven by an internal combustion engine. And just who invented such a machine is, to say the least, open to argument.

It clarifies matters only a little to take the various steps in the development of the modern motor car chronologically. If we do, we find that the man who first *thought* of it was the great Isaac Newton who, in 1688, almost a hundred years before Cugnot's steam carriage, designed a *jet-engined* horseless carriage. It was never built.

Other inventors turned to steam, but it was not until 1804 that Isaac de Rivaz designed an internal combustion engine relying upon hydrogen gas. Robert Street, an Englishman, and Philippe le Bon, another Frenchman, also patented internal combustion engines in 1794 and 1797 respectively.

None of these inventors, however, installed an engine into a horseless carriage. That honour seems to

An early advertisement for Daimler cars. Although Karl Benz was the first manufacturer to sell cars to the public in any quantity, Daimlers subsequently took the lead when Benz failed to expand. Eventually the two firms merged.

belong indisputably to a man who has been virtually ignored by motoring historians, an Englishman named Sam Brown. Sam Brown was an engineer who, in 1823, designed and built a pumping engine for a number of London waterworks. The engine was derived from the Newcomen-type of condensing steam engine, but used ordinary coal-gas for fuel.

Three years later, in 1826, Brown adapted this engine to propel a road vehicle. On 27 May he wheeled out his vehicle for a road test. It was a large but stumpy vehicle, nearly as wide as it was long, with 4 wooden wheels, each 1.5 m (5 ft) in diameter. The engine was gigantic and today would be described as a 40-litre engine. The mixture was carefully regulated so no actual explosion occurred and there was simply a burning away of gas. Nevertheless, it was undoubtedly an internal combustion engine. Some detractors have declared that it used coal-gas, but they are confused by Brown's waterworks engines. His road vehicle ran on commercial alcohol and disbelievers can look up the details in the British Patents Office, where Brown's plans and specifications are still preserved.

The scene for Brown's road test was Shooters Hill, in south-east London, a very steep hill which would provide a severe test for any vehicle. Brown himself, like many inventors and engineers a modest man, has left no account of his hill-climb but, according to an eye-witness account by a Mr J.A. Whitfield, of the Bedlington Iron Works, the feat was accomplished with the greatest of ease.

Unfortunately for Brown, steam was all the rage, and, in fact, there were no developments of the motor car until the 1860s. Steam buses and coaches were already on the roads and the great railway age was about to dawn. Brown's 'motor car', although a practical proposition as he had demonstrated, was slow compared with the steam vehicles. So Brown dropped further development in this field and turned to motor boats, of which he became a successful designer and manufacturer.

Samuel Brown has never been given the credit due him: *the honour of having designed and built and driven the first automobile propelled by any power other than steam.*

Although Brown's vehicle worked well, it is generally thought that, without an actual explosion, the engine could have produced little power: the ex-

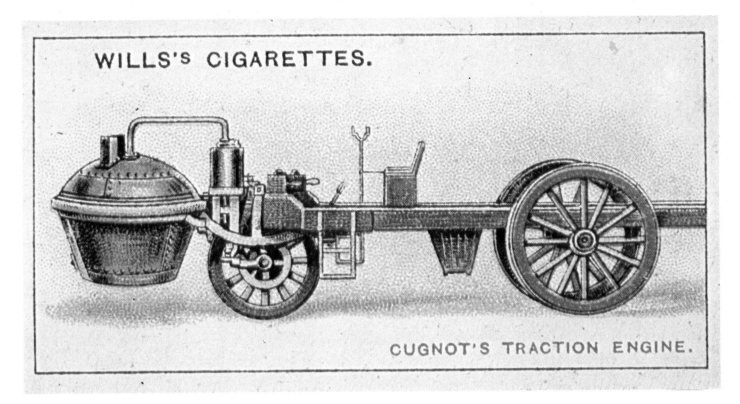

WILLS'S CIGARETTES.

CUGNOT'S TRACTION ENGINE.

Above: Steam dominated 18th-century transport, both by road and rail. The cigarette card depicts the steam gun-carriage designed by Cugnot which is generally regarded as the world's first successful horseless carriage. Left: Inventors followed up with many practical applications like the early London steam coach.

plosion of gas is necessary to drive the pistons in the engine and power results from the movement of these pistons. The first man to build such an engine was the Frenchman, Jean Etienne Lenoir, who produced a successful gas engine in 1860. It was very much like a steam engine, with a steam-engine type of valve admitting a mixture of coal-gas and air to each end of the cylinder alternately. There it was fired by an electric spark supplied by the batteries.

Because there was no attempt to compress the inflammable mixture in the cylinder before it was fired, it is generally assumed by engineers today that Lenoir's engine was very efficient. But when he fitted it into a carriage in 1862, the vehicle is reported to have travelled under its own power from Paris to Joinville-le-Pont and back, a distance of approximately 9.6 km (6 miles). Lenoir failed to see the possibilities of his invention and, like Brown before him, subsequently devoted his energies to motor boats and also to stationary engines, one of which is now in the Science Museum, London.

Thus Lenoir has the honour of being the first man to fit a true combustion engine, inasmuch as an actual explosion took place, into a self-propelled vehicle.

Meanwhile in Vienna, Siegfried Marcus, an engineer by training and an inventor by inclination, had the idea of making a gadget which would produce an explosive gas from liquid, in other words, a carburettor. He followed this through to complete an engine on internal combustion principles, using benzine as fuel.

Marcus contemplated fitting his engine to an airship, which obviously presented tremendous problems. While considering these, it occurred to him that if his engine could power an airship, it certainly ought to be able to propel a horseless carriage. Marcus bought a four-wheeled handcart, removed the rear wheels, fitted the engine and replaced the rear wheels, coupling them to the engine. There was one snag. As the rear wheels were, in effect, the flywheels of the engine, the entire contraption had to be lifted at the rear before the engine could be started.

Marcus continued to work on the machine and the following year, 1865, he felt that it was far enough advanced for him to invite some friends to ride in the vehicle. He chose a road which led to the Schmelz Cemetery for the test runs. It was quiet and seldom used, but, being little more than a rutted cart-track, it was hardly ideal for testing automobiles. Waiting until after dark in order to attract as little attention as possible, Marcus and his friends set off, one man pulling the machine, Marcus and another pushing.

Starting the engine after arriving at the cemetery road was quite a task, but eventually it fired and Marcus and his friends jumped aboard. It was a short-lived triumph. The handcart ran forward for a couple of hundred yards, there was a sudden crack, and it came to a halt. Nothing Marcus could do would make it work again, and so it was a dispirited party which returned home as they had come, pulling and pushing the vehicle.

Marcus continued his experiments and by 1868 had produced a modified version of his automobile. He worked, too, on the automobile which was displayed at the Vienna Exhibition of 1873, although it had yet to run. Finally, one night in 1875, Marcus decided the machine was ready for a real test – a journey to Klosterneuburg, nearly 12.8 km (8 miles) away.

According to contemporary accounts, the trial run caused a great commotion. The noise of the engine bursting into life caused neighbours to throw up their windows, demanding to know what was going on. One did his best to dampen the proceedings by throwing a bucket of water at Marcus and his friend.

They moved off. The second Marcus vehicle had a number of improvements, including rubber buffers fitted to the rear-axle to give a better 'ride'. Even so, the machine jolted along the none-too-smooth highway, the single cylinder engine thumped and thundered, coughed and spluttered, the iron tyres screeched and clattered, the wooden body groaned and squeaked. Yet it kept going, attaining a top speed of 6 kph (4 mph) before reaching Klosterneuburg where Marcus brought the machine to a halt by applying the block brake.

The return journey to Vienna was made without incident, and Marcus continued his trials. However, although he took great care to only use the automobile when the streets were comparatively deserted, many complaints were made by people whose sleep had been disturbed.

One day the police called. Marcus was told in no uncertain terms that he must desist. His activities were disturbing people's rest, frightening little children and horses and when the crowds gathered around him, the pickpockets got busy. Marcus heeded the warning. He only made four vehicles.

Yet his work did not go unheeded. One Marcus automobile went to Holland and interested manufacturers there, another to the United States where it was seen by a young man named Henry Ford and a third is displayed at the Vienna Technical Museum. Using surgical spirit for fuel, the curator still drives it occasionally – proof of the practicality of the design.

Marcus undoubtedly produced a practical automobile, but his place in history would be more secure had he persevered for longer than he did.

Below: The Bollée family, father and sons, were leading pioneers of the horseless carriage and one of their early ventures was this steam carriage, built in 1877. Right: A front-page from a French newspaper, *Le Petit Journal,* **which was to the forefront in championing the horseless carriage.**

Le Petit Journal

TOUS LES JOURS
Le Petit Journal
5 Centimes

SUPPLÉMENT ILLUSTRÉ
Huit pages : CINQ centimes

TOUS LES DIMANCHES
Le Supplément illustré
5 Centimes

Cinquième année   LUNDI 6 AOUT 1894   Numéro 194

Concours au « Petit Journal »

LES VOITURES SANS CHEVAUX

11

Above: The start of it all: rear and front views of the Benz motorized tricycle of 1885. Below: Daimler's original Quadricycle as shown at the International Exhibition in Paris in 1889.

Not generally known is the fact that about the time Marcus was making successful runs in his car, far away in Australia a Mr Blackburn invented a mechanical road vehicle which, although quite unlike any other, surely earns its inventor a place in the history of the motor car.

The machine was described in the *Sydney Mail* in February, 1879:

The motive power is obtained by the combustion of benzoline, a small jet of which is admitted into the burner. It is then set on fire, and is completely consumed by a current of air, which, until the machine is in action, is produced by turning a small handle. . . .

The burner, about the size of an ordinary chimney-pot hat, and quite as elegant, is lined by coils of a copper tube containing water; this tube is calculated to bear 2,000 pounds on the square inch, and in working receives only 60 pounds; so that practically, it is not likely to burst, and if such accident did occur, the results would not be serious, as the whole tube contains only one pound of water.

The steam generated in this tube passes at one end into the cylinders of a small torpedo engine, which rotates a horizontal shaft; it then passes into a cooler where it is condensed by the effect of a current of cold air driven against the outside of the vessel by a revolving fan, and the water so produced is forced back into the other end of the tubular boiler by a force pump; hence, there is not the slightest escape of steam, nor is there any smoke, as the benzoline is entirely consumed by the current of air.

The revolving engine shaft works the driving shaft: not directly, but by the medium of two cones placed side by side, their bases being reversed in position. A figure of 8 band connects the two and, as it nears the base of one it moves towards the apex of the other and thus increases or diminishes the speed of the driving shaft, which is connected with the drivingwheel, or off-wheel, by an endless band.

It was claimed for Blackburn's invention that it would do 12.8 kph (8 mph) on the level ground and 6.4 kph (4 mph) up moderate hills. In one way he was not very forward-looking – the vehicle was steered by reins, in exactly the same way as a horse carriage. But he was far ahead of his time in having one-pedal control.

The evidence is strong that Blackburn's carriage not only existed but worked. The report in the *Sydney Mail* was based upon an earlier report by W.B. Tegetmier, published in the *Field* in 1878, and this, in turn, was republished in *The South Australian Motor* in 1928 and again in that most reliable of organs, *Veteran Car*, in 1978.

While other countries rage and rant over the invention of the motor car, there is a certain piquancy in thinking that an obscure Australian was inventing away with the best of them.

The continuing police ban on Marcus's efforts and Mr Blackburn's experiments notwithstanding, caused the development of the motor car to switch to Germany where, in 1872, Dr N.A. Otto had devised a 'silent gas engine'. The 4-stroke operating cycle he produced was to be the basis of the majority of engines subsequently used in the automobile industry. Otto thus set the scene for the two men who were to have the greatest impact on the early history of the motor car, Karl Benz and Gottlieb Daimler.

Benz, a manufacturer of small gas engines, had cherished the idea of designing and building a self-propelled vehicle since his student days. Eventually, Fate sent him a backer, a man named Max Rose. The first Benz machine was a motor-cycle, a primitive effort which was little more than a 'bone-shaker' bicycle fitted with a small gas engine. It was a flop. By 1885 his first car was ready for trial. It was something like an overgrown bath-chair, with two large wheels at the rear and a smaller pivoted one in front which was operated by a tiller, thus steering the machine. The engine was behind the seat (which held the driver and one passenger) and between the two rear wheels. Unlike Marcus's machine in which the rear wheels acted as flywheels, Benz fitted one horizontal flywheel, the idea being to prevent interference with the steering when cornering.

It was driven for the first time in the spring of 1885

Below: The Comte De Dion, one of the French pioneers of automobilism, astride one of his own steam tricycles. More De Dions take part in the famous Brighton Run than any other make. Bottom: A 1904 Stanley Steamer, another fine car of the period.

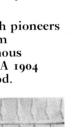

13

when the inventor took it around the cinder track surrounding his factory. It appeared on the public highway in October, ten years after the Marcus automobile had appeared on the streets of Vienna. The first run in public was far from trouble-free and the machine had to be pushed back to the factory amid hoots and jeers. A week or two later, Benz succeeded in travelling about half-a-mile at 8 mph. He then fitted a more powerful engine, wooden wheels, and a second speed to enable easier starting and climbing of gradients.

He set himself a target: a non-stop run around Mannheim in two circuits. It took dozens of attempts but Benz would not give up and one magic day the run was completed without trouble. The age of the motor car had dawned because weird as the Benz contraption may have looked it was the forerunner of most modern cars, water-cooled with a differential gear and electric ignition.

From then on, Benz concentrated on the manufacture of cars, the first man to build such machines

for sale to the general public. In all his efforts, he had had the unwavering support of his wife, Bertha, and sons, Eugen and Richard. In 1888, this remarkable woman and her boys were to make the first really significant car journey in the world. They drove from Mannheim to Pforzheim, Bertha's hometown, a distance of 96.5 km (60 miles), an epoch-making event which proved the real practicability of the motor car. There were no petrol stations or garages along the way so they obtained fuel from chemists' shops, and a shoemaker at Bauchlott renewed the leather for the brake-shoes. A blockage in the petrol flow to the carburettor was cleared with Bertha's hatpin, and a short-circuit in the electrical system was overcome with a garter. When they reached steepish hills, she

and 15-year-old Eugen pushed while 13-year-old Richard steered. Bertha Benz was certainly a remarkable woman.

And her husband was undoubtedly the father of the automobile industry.

Meanwhile, working without knowledge of the work of Benz, Daimler built a petrol driven motor cycle in 1885 and a four-wheeled car in 1886.

He, his partner Wilhelm Maybach and the clever French designer, Emil Levassor, were eventually to outstrip Benz in the production of new and better automobiles and *it is mainly due to them that the industry grew in leaps and bounds.*

Panhard and Levassor in France, Simms and others in Great Britain, obtained the Daimler rights for their countries and the automobile boom was under way.

Denmark also lays claim to producing an automobile around the same time as Benz and Daimler,

the Hammel, in 1886. Many years later this car took part in the famous London to Brighton Run but many historians were reluctant to accept its date as 1886. In any case, Mr Hammel deserves little of the credit – the car was apparently designed and built by his blacksmith, one Hans Urban Johansen.

There is little controversy about the innovators of the motor car in the rest of Europe. In France, in 1890, the Daimler-based Panhards started the great French industry which was to be perpetuated by Renault, Peugeot, Citroën, Delahaye, Delage, Darracq, Talbot and others.

In Great Britain, Edward Butler, who had exhibited drawings of a motor tricycle in 1884, finally produced one in 1889. In 1892, Roots and Venables engines were fitted in Coventry tricycles, and in 1894 a Walthamstow builder, Frederick Bremer, constructed a car which was little more than a soap-box on wheels.

It is on exhibition in the Walthamstow Museum, London, and in the 1960s participated in the Brighton Run. In 1895 John Henry Knight constructed a car which has been widely-hailed as the first British car. None of these really made an impact and it was left to the Lanchesters, Austins, Rolls and Royces, to create the British automobile industry.

In the US, however, the argument still rages as to who was the father of the American automobile.

Selden claimed to have filed the first patents for a motor car in 1879, but he was a shrewd lawyer who tried to patent everything possible in connection with horseless carriages so that, if they ever became a practical proposition, he could collect royalties from *all* the manufacturers.

Many history books credit the first petrol-driven car built in the United States to the brothers, Charles and Frank Duryea. First driven through the streets of Springfield, Massachusetts, in 1893, the Duryea is preserved in the National Museum, Washington.

For many years Elwood Haynes was a rival claimant to this honour, but more recent research has 'discovered' a man with a more genuine claim.

John William Lambert was a mechanical genius who invented the first automatic corn-planter, and there is sworn evidence that he drove a gasoline-powered automobile on the main street of Ohio City more than a year before the Duryeas produced their first successful automobile. As no customers were forthcoming for his car, Lambert readily agreed when a friend, Elwood Haynes, asked permission to advertise the Haynes as the first American car.

In later years he stayed out of the controversy as to who was first, although he resumed car manufacture with the Union and the Buckeye. The Lambert firm still exists, manufacturing automotive and other industrial parts and there are still a number of Lambert cars in existence. Lambert patented more than 600 inventions, most of them connected with automobiles, including a gearless, friction-drive car which he began manufacturing in 1900.

His right to be the first American car-builder is upheld by one James A. Swoveland, who said:

I rode with Mr. Lambert in this first car on the streets of Ohio City in the summer of 1891. I recall that there were still stumps in the dirt street and Mr. Lambert had to maneuver the car in order to avoid hitting those stumps. On one occasion he did hit the roots of one which made the car skid into a hitching-rack. A number of men helped us pull the car backward and we then continued on our way. . . . The car had two large wheels at the rear and a smaller one at the front center. It was steered by a lever. It had a fringed top.

Henry Ford was not concerned in the Lambert-Haynes-Duryea controversy as he did not build his first car until 1896. He was, however, to emerge not only as *the true father of the American automobile industry, but also as a key figure in spreading that industry world-wide.*

Left: The White was another successful American steam car.

Below: Completing a trio of outstanding American steam cars is the Locomobile. Several examples of this excellent car survive today.

The Trail blazers

Henry Ford was a truly remarkable man although apparently not a very lovable one. Nevertheless, there is no law that says geniuses must be lovable, and Ford, his works, his descendants and his successors have made an indelible mark on the automobile industry and consequently on the life and economic conditions of the twentieth century.

He dreamed – many years before Hitler – of a car for the masses. As early as 1905 he built a roadster which sold for $500 (£100), a comparatively modest sum. Three years later the first Model-T Ford was on the market. It broke away from copying European models and switched the driving-seat to the left-hand side of the car, the logical place in a country where cars were driven on the right-hand side of the road.

Left: One of the world's most famous cars, a 1912 Model T Ford Convertible Tourer. Below: A great car of the period was the 1909 Thomas Flyer, with many record-breaking achievements to its credit.

The Model-T was cheaper than its competitors and more economical to run, but it had a lukewarm welcome. Ford had used lightweight steel alloy in its manufacture. Unsafe, cried the pundits. The car was modest in price. How could he do it? There must be something wrong with the car, scoffed the sceptics. More miles to the gallon? Prove it, sneered the cynics.

Henry Ford was determined to do just that. Never afraid to take a chance, he was an early believer in the influence of motor sport on the sales of cars, a dictum which remains true of the Ford Motor Company today. And he was about to get an excellent opportunity to show what his cars could do.

Robert Guggenheim, a mining millionaire, had offered a trophy and prize-money for the first car to 'blaze a trail' from New York to Puget Sound, a distance of more than 6,436 km (4,000 miles). The Alaskan-Yukon-Pacific Exposition was being held in Seattle and it was felt that the future prosperity of the region demanded the exploration and development of

every possible means of communication between East and West, including roads.

Many parts of the route were just trails; other sections did not even appear on the map. And two cars, sent to ascertain if the contest was possible, failed to complete the journey, at least by road. One got there aboard a freight train and the other expired in the backwoods of Idaho.

Despite this the contest went ahead. Ford entered two Model-T's, one to be driven by Frank Kulick and H.B. Harper, the other by Bert Scott and C.J. Smith. They were up against an Itala, a Shawmut and an Acme. The rules were strict: contestants would only be allowed to obtain spare parts at two places on the long journey, Chicago and Cheyenne, and flanged wheels could not be carried. The organizers had no intention of letting some slick operator travel along the railway tracks when the going got tough.

President Taft himself was there when the cars set off from City Hall, New York, on 1 June, 1909. The cars coped fairly comfortably as far as St Louis, but trouble lay ahead. Storms had swept the country for more than a week and the further the cars went, the worse the conditions became. Roads were a quagmire, streams raging torrents and bridges had succumbed to the battering of the raging waters. Detours had to be made, adding miles to the already long journey. Time after time, the cars stuck, bogged down in mud up to the axles. In these conditions, the Ford crews were

Previous pages: A car passing through an English village. Front page of a catalogue for Peugeot cars (above). Right: A 1903 Mercedes. Inset: The Hon. C.S. Rolls in the Panhard which won the 1896 Paris-Marseilles race, the first four-cylinder Panhard ever built.

grateful for the comparative lightness of their machines which never settled in the mud as heavily as their competitors and were easier to push out.

In modern times, much of the Ford reputation has been built on the availability of service and spares. It all began in that Guggenheim Trophy with a chain of Ford agents dotted strategically across the country. Although forbidden to provide spares, the Ford agents were able to help the works cars in a variety of ways and the crews were never short of a hot meal and a hot bath which sent them, refreshed, on their way.

The cars battled on, but at Cheyenne disappointment awaited the crew of the Itala. A wire from the owner of the car ordered them to abandon the contest and ship his precious car to the Exposition by train. Newspaper accounts of the race had convinced him that his beloved car would not reach Seattle in one piece if allowed to continue.

The four surviving cars still had nearly 1,609 km (1,000 miles) to cover, part of it through Wyoming, a tract of 100,000 square miles which, even 50 years later, could only boast 160 townships with a popu-

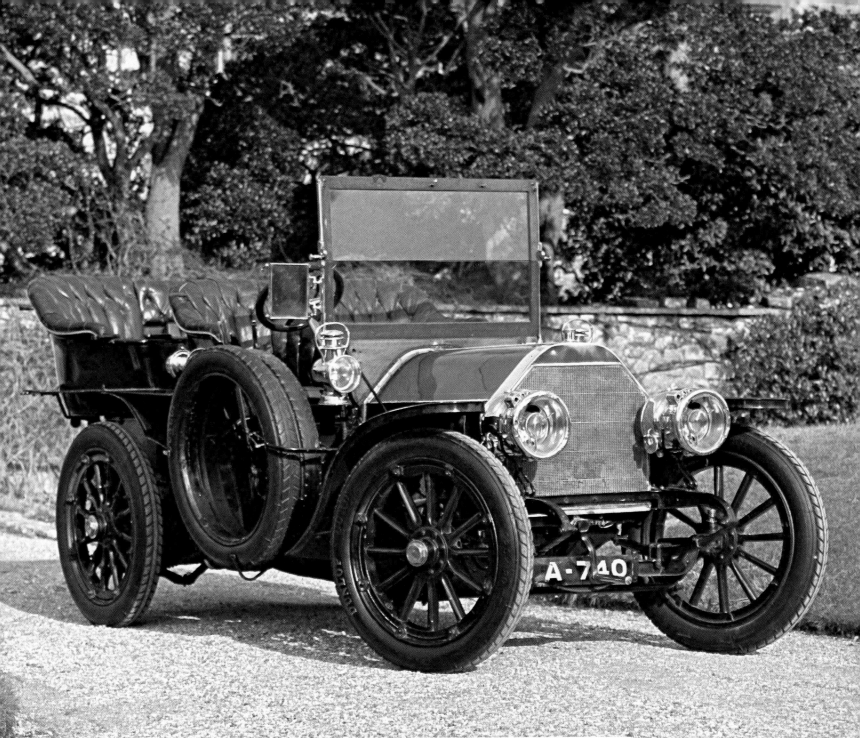

Below and right: The perils which confronted the early motorist. The American millionaire, William Vanderbilt, meets with an accident in Italy and is attacked by peasants who, whatever their nationality, tended to take a dim view of these 'noisy, stinking machines which frighten the horses'. Vanderbilt was one of the founders of modern auto racing.

Far right: Walter C. Bersey's electric landau on 'Emancipation Day', 1896, the first London to Brighton Run.

lation of more than 100. It was rough, tough country through which the cars struggled. Across Idaho, briefly into Oregon and finally into Washington. Seattle was close at hand now. Close – but barred from the cars by the Cascade Mountains. And no car had yet managed the Snoqualmie Pass which led through the mountains. Although it was nearly July, the snow still lay thick and deep in the Cascades.

It was just another obstacle to be overcome as far as Henry Ford was concerned. He hired a gang of men, bought some shovels and led the way into the mountains. Ford No. 2 was leading the race, with Scott and Smith, and Henry and his gang went ahead of it, digging a path through the deepest snowdrifts, Henry wielding a shovel with the best of them. Behind them, Kulick, Ford's No. 1 driver, was in trouble, his car having hit a rock hidden by the snow. He and Harper had no alternative but to get to work to repair the damage as best they could.

Meanwhile, No. 2, thanks to Henry, was clear of the Cascades and driving into Seattle in triumph, Scott at the wheel. The Model-T had covered the 6,607 km

(4,106 miles) in 22 days 55 minutes, and it still had New York air in at least two of its tyres.

At the victory banquet, Guggenheim handed over his trophy with the words,

'Mr Ford's theory that a lightweight car, highly powered for its weight, can go places where heavier cars cannot go and can beat heavier cars costing five and six times as much on the steep hills or on bad roads, has been proved. I believe Mr Ford has the solution of the problem of the popular automobile.'

And he had. 'Henry's Tin Lizzie', a term coined in derision, became an affectionate slogan which slipped into American history. The Model-T, modified but little through the years, had sold fifteen million by 1927. The Model-T was not just a car, it was a symbol of a new age. No other car in the history of the automobile, not even England's well-loved 'Baby Austin' or the much-later 'Mini', ever held such a place in the affections of a nation as Henry's Tin Lizzie, the car which really started on its climb to fame the day its designer toiled up a mountain pass with a shovel.

The Guggenheim Trophy was not a unique event at the time. It had been preceded in 1907 by a great race from Peking to Paris and in 1908 by a 'Round The World' Race, won by the American Thomas Flyer.

Peking to Paris was promoted by the French newspaper, *Le Matin*, which claimed that it was not to be a race. There would be no regulations and all cars which succeeded in covering the 16,090 km (10,000

25

mile) route would be deemed to have accomplished performances of equal merit. The route would be via the Gobi Desert through Siberia to Irkutsk and Moscow, and a camel caravan was dispatched from Peking to cache petrol at various points along the way.

The entry-list was a formidable one but, as the start drew near, many of the potential contestants thought better of it and withdrew, leaving only five cars to face the starter on 10 June, 1907.

There were two works De Dion Boutons, driven by Cormier and Collignon, a privately-entered Itala, with Prince Scipione Borghese at the wheel, Goddard in a works Spyker from Holland, and a spidery little works Contal, driven by Pons.

Hardly had they left Peking, bound for Nankow, than the rains came and in the first three days the cars covered barely 129 km (80 miles). Conditions were bad for the giant Itala, but for the little Contal they were well-nigh impossible. Fed-up with digging his car out of the mud and deserted by his coolies, Pons resigned himself to the inevitable and sent his car ahead by train.

The others kept going alongside the Great Wall of China to the awesome plains of Mongolia. The Itala was now well in front and reached Urga, the capital of Mongolia, in fine style. Later they were seriously delayed when the car stuck in a bog, but eventually they got through to Siberia where they made good time along the unsleepered tracks of the Trans-Siberia Railway. Ferried across the Volga by the boatmen of song and legend, Borghese and his companions, Barzini and Guizzardi, drove into Moscow with an escort of Cossacks.

When they reached St Petersburg they were greeted by a cavalcade of ten cars, the leading one an American Buick with two pioneer autocarists, Kritch, a Russian, and Walter Windham, an Englishman, aboard. Two months after they left Peking, the Italians drove into Paris to be hailed as conquering heroes. The robust Itala, it was said, must be preserved in perpetuity as a memorial to the ingenuity of automobile engineers.

Two weeks later, Cormier and Collignon arrived in Paris in the De Dions, accompanied by Goddard's mechanic in the Spyker, Goddard having retired from the fray and taken to the railway. They too were greeted like heroes, as indeed they were.

French manufacturers caught the enthusiasm and, as a result, Panhard, Mors, De Dietrich, Peugeot and Bollée were almost household names. In Great Britain, however, no one had yet thought it worthwhile to set up as a manufacturer and most of the petrol-driven vehicles on the road were imported from France and Germany. The Light Locomotive Act of 1865, although amended somewhat in 1878, restricted vehicles to 6.4 kph (4 mph), reducible by Local Government Boards to 3.2 kph (2 mph).

In 1896, British law was amended again. The speed limit was increased to 19 kph (12 mph) and the requirement that vehicles should be preceded by a pedestrian was rescinded.

To celebrate the 'emancipation' of the motorist, an entrepreneur named Harry J. Lawson organized a run from London to Brighton. It was an illustrious occasion. The great Gottlieb Daimler came over to ride in one of the cars and Bollée sent over a team of three cars from France. The Duke of Saxe-Weimar, the Earl of Winchilsea and the author, Jerome K. Jerome, all attended the start. There were two Duryeas from the USA and a Panhard which had achieved great things in the Paris–Marseilles race. In all, 39 cars started.

Reportedly, 14 of these finished the Run, although it is believed that the owner of one of the electric cars put his machine aboard the train, unloaded it at Preston Park, just outside Brighton, bespattered the car with mud to make it appear authentic and drove the remaining few miles to the finish. Certainly, of those which did get there under their own power, two were the Bollées driven by Leon and Camille Bollée, H.O. Duncan having come to grief in the third works car, and the Panhards of Mayade and Mayer, the latter with Lawson aboard.

A hopeful gleam, but no more than that, for the future British motor industry was that an Arnold Motor Carriage also finished. The Arnold was derived from the Benz, Walter Arnold being the English concessionaire of the German firm. This same Arnold was still being successfully driven in the Brighton Run 70 years later.

Yet although the Run is celebrated annually and attracts hundreds of thousands of spectators and cars from all over the world, the Thousand Miles Trial of 1900 played a more important role in establishing the motor car in Britain.

Devised by the fertile brain of the newspaper tycoon Alfred Harmsworth, later Lord Northcliffe, and organized by the infant Automobile Club of Great Britain and Ireland, now the RAC, the Trial took the motor car to parts of the country where such a vehicle had never been seen before. At all major halts there were displays and competitions and for the first time the population was made aware of the tremendous potential of the petrol-driven horseless carriage.

One driver who acquitted himself particularly well was the Hon. C.S. Rolls who was soon to become associated with Henry Royce in producing the world's most famous car, the Rolls-Royce.

The motor car was on its way. . . .

An advertisement of the British Daimler Motor Company, proudly boasting of their Royal patronage. For many years, the Royal Family used Daimler cars exclusively.

Daimler

HER MAJESTY THE QUEEN has graciously accorded the Daimler Company permission to exhibit at their London Showrooms, 27-28, Pall Mall, during the Olympia Show Week, her new 38 H.P. Daimler with Hooper body.

The Birmingham Small Arms Co., Ltd.,
The Daimler Motor Co. (1904), Ltd., } AMALGAMATED.

The Early Racers

If there is a motoring Valhalla then it is likely that two Frenchmen, the Comte de Dion and Emile Levassor, are still arguing over who won the world's first motor race. Certainly, the sport's many historians have never ceased to debate the issue: De Dion in 1894 or Levassor in 1895? Official sources do not credit either of them – which just adds another complication to a tangled skein.

What happened was this:

Late in December, 1893, the French newspaper, *Le Petit Journal*, announced that the following summer it would organize a competition. Entries flowed in and on 22 June, 1894, the historic event duly took place.

The route was from Paris to Rouen, a distance of 126 km (78.5 miles), but there were frequent halts while the cars were put on public display and the drivers obtained refreshment. It was this aspect of the event which bolstered the contentions of those who claimed it was a rally and not a race. Nevertheless, it had been announced as a competition and results were issued by the organizers.

The first car to reach Rouen was a De Dion 'Steam-drag' driven by the Comte de Dion at an average speed of 18.7 kph (11.6 mph) and it seems hard on him that both his contemporaries and subsequent historians have tried to rob him of the unique distinction of winning the world's first motor race. For the organizers did not, in fact, award him first prize. His car, it was said, did not altogether comply with the rules of the competition and so honours were shared between a Panhard and a Peugeot, both driven by $3\frac{1}{2}$-horsepower petrol engines.

Marcel Renault in the ill-fated 1903 Paris-Madrid race in which he was one of many people killed.

PARIS-VIENNE 1902

GUILLAUME sur DARRACQ

Race or rally, Paris to Rouen had literally set the wheels in motion and plans were laid for what would indisputably be a race the following year, from Paris to Bordeaux and back to the French capital, a distance of 1,178 km (732 miles). Such a tremendous distance over public roads involved many organizational problems and a committee was set up to deal with them. This led in turn to the formation of the Automobile Club de France, the world's first motoring organization, which was to be followed in 1897 by the Automobile Club of Great Britain and Ireland, now the RAC.

Twenty cars started in the Paris–Bordeaux race, 13 petrol-driven, 6 steam and 1 electric, and 9 finished, 8 of them petrol-driven and the other a Bollée steamer.

First man home on 13 June, 1895, was Emile Levassor. He drove his Panhard single-handed for 48 hours and 48 minutes at an average speed of 24 kph (15 mph), a magnificent feat for the time and the circumstances. A big factor in his success was his car's reliability. Other competitors had frequent breakdowns, but Levassor's Panhard kept going, and he had only one enforced stop which cost him 22 minutes.

Like the Comte de Dion before him, Levassor did not get official credit for his win. The regulations specified that cars should have seats for four persons – and the Panhard had only two. So the official winner was a Peugeot which had been the third to finish.

Unlike the Count, however, Levassor was publicly acclaimed as the winner then – and now. So posterity seems to be on Emile's side. But, whatever the rights and wrongs of these results, in Europe a pattern of racing had now been established on a town-to-town, city-to-city basis, which was to last for some years.

The Michelin building in London has many decorative tiles depicting great moments in motoring history. The one above is of the 1902 Paris-Vienna race and features the French driver, Guillaume, in his Darracq.

Meanwhile, the Americans, impressed by the French event, launched one of their own, designed, it was said, to test the speed and stamina of American-made cars. Organized by the *Chicago Times Herald*, it was a modest affair of 87.47 km (54.36 miles), from the centre of Chicago to the suburbs and back and was won by J. Frank Duryea in a car of his own manufacture. The winning speed was 12 kph (7.5 mph), which was better than it sounds in view of the slush and snow which covered the city. The date was 28 November, 1895.

In 1896, a Bollée won the Paris–Trouville race at 45.4 kph (28.2 mph), a winning speed which would not be exceeded in any race for another three years. Michelin had introduced pneumatic tyres for racing in 1895 and persevered with them despite much criticism and many teething troubles. He was duly rewarded, and by 1898 many cars had switched from solid tyres to pneumatics in order to cope with ever-rising speeds.

Panhards introduced wheel-steering, a grim result of the death of the firm's head, the great Levassor, who never recovered from a crash resulting from the previously universal tiller steering.

With cars now of all shapes and sizes, race organizers began to make regulations dividing events into classes according to weight, size of engine and so on. Stricter control of races also became necessary, and in 1899 flag marshals were first employed to signal instructions to competing drivers.

Stamina, as well as speed, was being demanded of the racers and in 1899, the Chevalier René de Knyff won the Tour de France, a distance of 2,172 km (1,350 miles), in a $4\frac{1}{2}$-litre Panhard, at an average speed of 48.6 kph (30.2 mph). An absolutely fantastic achievement on the primitive roads of the time.

By the following year the racing Panhards had grown to $7\frac{1}{2}$-litres and weighed well over a ton. Their bitter rivals, the Mors, were even bigger, with 10-litre engines, and in 1900, for the very first time, they wrested the honours from Panhard in the Paris–Bordeaux race.

A new event now appeared on the scene, the International Cup, or, as it became better-known, the Gordon Bennett Race. James Gordon Bennett, an American newspaper proprietor living in Paris, presented a trophy for competition amongst cars nominated by the national automobile clubs of each country. The first race in the series, in 1900, was something of a damp squib. It was run from Paris to Lyons, a distance of 568.54 km (353.35 miles), and only five cars were entered: the official French team of three Panhards with De Knyff, Charron and Girardot at the controls; Camille Jenatzy in a Belgium Snoeck-Bolide; and Alexander Winton, representing the USA in one of his own cars. Only two of the Panhards finished, Charron crossing the line, with a speed of 62.1 kph (38.6 mph), more than an hour ahead of his team-mate Girardot.

The organizers decided to run the 1901 Gordon Bennett Race in conjunction with the Paris–Bordeaux event. It was just as well. Despite all sorts of bold challenges from various countries, only the French entries actually started, two Panhards driven by Charron and Girardot and a Mors handled by Levegh. Girardot, who finished tenth overall in the concurrently run Paris–Bordeaux, was declared winner of the Gordon Bennett Trophy at an average speed of 59.5 kph (37 mph).

The future looked far from bright for the brainchild of the owner of the *New York Herald Tribune*, but motor-racing had far more to worry about. In the Paris to Berlin race which came next in the calendar, Brazier, driving a Mors, hit and killed a small boy. The government announced that no more racing would be permitted on French roads.

The arguments which followed between conflicting interests were long and complex. Suffice it to say that the ban did not last and the Gordon Bennett Race was again run in 1902, this time in conjunction with the Paris–Vienna Race which attracted a record 219 entries. The Gordon Bennett entry, of course, was of much more modest proportions, but at least this time the French were faced with a challenge from a British team comprising two Wolseleys and a Napier, the last driven by S.F. Edge. The Wolseleys experienced all sorts of troubles and although one of them did

eventually cover a good section of the route, controls were closed when it arrived and so, like its companion car, it was not even officially classed as a starter. Thus Edge, whose chances were regarded as hopeless, was left to play a lone hand against the previous year's winner, Girardot, this time in a CGV, Fournier in a Mors and De Knyff in a Panhard.

The start was from Champigny in the small hours of 26 June, the Gordon Bennett competitors preceding the rest of the field. Girardot was first to leave, followed by Fournier, Edge and De Knyff. Fournier went like the proverbial bomb, but his explosive rush soon expired when the clutch-shaft of his Mors broke. Girardot also retired with a split petrol tank and so, at this early stage, the Gordon Bennett had narrowed down to a man-to-man fight between De Knyff and Edge. The Englishman's chances still looked slender, for at the completion of the first stage of the race De Knyff's Panhard was not only well in front of the Napier but also ahead of Charles Jarrott and Henry Farman who were competing in the Paris–Vienna race proper.

The next stage of the race was through Switzerland where there was a strong anti-motor-racing lobby. Consequently this stretch was neutralized, cars being limited to 24 kph (15 mph). There seemed not the slightest chance of Edge catching the Chevalier, but fate intervened and the differential casing-sleeve on the Panhard broke. The car struggled on but finally expired on the summit of Arlberg, leaving driver and mechanic to walk to the nearest village. Edge motored safely into Innsbruck to win the Gordon Bennett Trophy for England.

His green Napier had averaged 51.2 kph (31.8 mph) over the 565 km (351 miles) course, the lowest winning speed yet, but all were agreed that the route was the toughest ever.

The national automobile club of the winning country had the privilege of staging the Gordon Bennett Race the following year, and so for 1903 it was up to the Automobile Club of Great Britain and Ireland. But the anti-motoring forces were very strong in Britain and it seemed likely that the Club would have to relinquish its option. Fortunately, in 1902, the Belgians had demonstrated that there was a satisfactory alternative to racing on the open road by running the Circuit des Ardennes over roads closed to the public, an experiment repeated in 1903. The Belgian lead gave the Automobile Club its solution, and arrangements were made with the Irish authorities to run the 1903 Gordon Bennett over a circuit not far from Dublin.

Motor-racing's first big public relations effort paved the way. The Club circularized Irish MPs, newspapers, hoteliers, parish priests, mayors, landowners, local authorities and transport companies with their proposals. Several hundred letters were

Tiller steering contributed to many of the accidents in the early town-to-town races but in the Paris-Amsterdam race of 1898, the winner, Charron, drove a Panhard with a steering wheel and this method of steering was universally adopted thereafter.

despatched, pointing out the advantages the race would bring in trade and tourist business, guaranteeing safety measures and emphasizing that the event would be held on a public holiday other than a Sunday, thus avoiding interference with both business and church interests.

The reaction was almost entirely favourable and a Bill was rushed through Parliament authorizing the closure of roads to form the race circuit, exempting competing cars from speed limits and local authorities from calls on their funds for road improvements. The outlay involved had to be raised privately and by public appeal. There were other difficulties too; it was reported that some local authorities in Ireland did not even possess a steamroller.

Great Britain was to have a full representation of three cars. Two of the team virtually chose themselves: Edge, the previous year's winner, and Charles Jarrott, probably the outstanding British driver of the period, both on Napiers. Eliminating trials between other Napiers and Star machines were held to select the third entry and from these trials J.W. Stocks (Napier) was chosen.

Formal challenges for the Trophy came from France, Germany and the USA. The French team was a formidable one: De Knyff and Farman, both on Panhards, and Gabriel with a Mors. The Americans, after holding eliminating trials, nominated two Wintons, driven by Percy Owen and Winton himself, plus a Peerless with Louis Mooers at the wheel. From Germany came three 60-horsepower Mercedes, the three newly-constructed 90-hp cars having been burnt in a fire which gutted the Canstatt works. One of the German team's difficulties was that the German club would only permit amateur drivers and all the best German drivers of the time were professionals, inasmuch as they were employed by others, usually as mechanics or chauffeurs. So the men who were to uphold the honour of the Fatherland were two Belgians, Jenatzy and Baron de Caters, and an American, Foxhall-Keene.

Hopes were high for the British team following Edge's win and certainly the drivers, and their team manager, Montague Napier, took it seriously enough. The racing drivers of today may be interested in the British team's training methods: Edge indulged in the exercises advocated by the great wrestler and weight-lifter, Eugene Sandow, Jarrott and Stocks played cricket and Napier daily sluiced himself outdoors with cold water from a well.

Other aspects of the event were also rather different. Edge later recalled:

We had some amusing experiences with some of the Irish peasants. It appeared to be the rule in Ireland that most of the main roads should be used as farmyards for the breeding of chickens and cattle. On some occasions it was impossible to avoid running into a few chickens in which case we always stopped and settled on the spot with the owners. As, however, our honesty in this direction became known, we noticed a perceptibly greater number of chickens on certain sections of the course, with a correspondingly heavier death toll. We noticed too, that after these calamities, there was never the slightest difficulty in finding the owners at home and waiting for us. Another striking fact was that the value of the chickens became greater as time went on but no effort was made to present us with the corpses of the birds; we just paid up and went on.

The cars started at seven-minute intervals. Edge was first away, an appropriate honour, then came De Knyff, Owen, Jenatzy, Jarrott, Gabriel, Mooers, De Caters, Stocks, Farman and Foxhall-Keene. Winton had last-minute carburettor trouble and to qualify as a starter had to push his car over the line and then work on it for 40 minutes before he was able to get away. It was an omen. The Americans were never in the race and the British ran into trouble, Edge with his tyres, Jarrott crashing after steering trouble and Stocks, unluckiest of all, running into some loose wires left on the road after De Knyff had collided with the post holding them up.

France and Germany were left to fight it out and it was the latter country which scored its first International Cup victory, the Belgian 'Red Devil', Jenatzy, proving an easy winner at more than 80.5 kph (50 mph). He was followed home by the complete French team, in order: De Knyff, Farman and Gabriel, with Edge last, a long way behind.

The 1903 Gordon Bennett was not without significance in British motor-racing history. It had been well organized, attracted the best entry yet, was won in fine style by an outstanding driver and persuaded many people that there was something in motor-racing after all.

Alas for the immediate future of motor-racing, the Gordon Bennett was overshadowed by the race from Paris to Madrid which became known as 'The Race of Death'.

It was to be the greatest motor-race ever seen, as far as the organizers were concerned. The distance was 1,432 km (890 miles) and the entry-list included almost all of the world's outstanding drivers and cars. Public interest was fantastic. On the Saturday night before the race, thousands of men, women and children streamed along the road from Paris to

Inset: One of the many disasters in the 1903 Paris-Madrid race which had to be abandoned at Bordeaux and came to be known as 'The Race of Death'. Right: A 1903 De Dietrich which took part in the race.

34

Chartres where the race was to begin. In the city itself, hundreds of others flocked to the railway station at St Lazare, there to fill to overflowing the special trains which were being run. More than national prestige was at stake since every manufacturer taking part hoped for victory and a consequent boom in sales. Indeed, Charles Jarrott, who sold Napier and De Dietrich cars in his London showrooms, was advertising well before the event that his would be the first car to start.

The entries totalled an incredible 277 cars and motor-cycles of which no less than 216 actually started. Favourite was again De Knyff, in one of the 17 Panhards entered. Jarrott was to drive a De Dietrich, of which there were 10, one of them driven by a woman, Madame du Gast.

Jarrott was not the only British driver entered in a foreign car; Delaney and Barrow were also piloting De Dietrichs, while the Hon. C.S. Rolls, Du Cros and Holder had Panhards. There were five all-British entries: a Napier driven by Mayhew and a team of four Wolseleys with Girling, Porter, Cummings and Herbert (afterwards Lord) Austin as drivers.

The start was timed for 3.30 a.m. from Versailles, and it was estimated that something like 100,000 spectators gathered there. The procession of competitors was nearly a mile long and the luckless drivers at the back had to plough along as best they could through the clouds of dust raised by those in front.

Spectators milled around the cars and a half-battalion of engineers, armed with rifles, who had been drafted in to keep order, found their work cut out. There was so much confusion that the start was delayed for 15 minutes and, as each vehicle left the line, it had to nudge through a wall of spectators which immediately closed behind it. Fortunately, the crowd was reasonably good-tempered, except when the German entries appeared to shouts of 'A bas Mercedes'.

Jarrott, as his advertisements had promised, was first away but after 19.3 km (12 miles) found his clutch was slipping. His mechanic had to hold it in, releasing it as and when Jarrott required. Not surprisingly an ominous cloud of dust soon appeared behind them and De Knyff, the favourite and second man to start, swept past, followed by Louis Renault. The De Dietrich ground to a halt from fuel starvation and as Jarrott and his mechanic worked frantically, they expected that at any moment more would roar past. But none came. . . .

De Knyff's lead was short-lived and before the cars reached the first control at Chartres he was forced to retire with tyre trouble. Another fancied driver, Fournier, also had to drop out through magneto failure.

With the wisdom of hindsight, impending disaster seemed to loom everywhere. Although police were stationed every hundred yards or so along the route, they were powerless to control the crowds. People surged across the road, heedless of the dangers. A woman ran in front of one of the competitors causing him to crash. Another tried desperately to avoid a stray dog and the steering of his car, lightened to the point of weakness to save a few ounces, broke under the sudden strain.

As the leading cars approached Tours at the end of the second stage, the order remained Renault from Jarrott but then came a challenge from Werner in one of the new Mercedes. He roared past the Englishman in a cloud of dust, but grimly Jarrott hung on and just the other side of Tours the German's back-axle broke.

Jarrott was back in second place, but Renault was now more than 30 minutes ahead and when the Englishman ran into more trouble, Jenatzy closed up on him. At the final control before Bordeaux, Jarrott heard that the 'Red Devil' was hard on his heels and was implored by fervently patriotic Frenchmen not to let the German Mercedes pass him.

Jarrott had more than nationalistic troubles on his mind. The wooden spokes of one of his front wheels had worked loose and his mechanic doused them with a bucket of water in the hope of swelling the spokes and making them tighten again. But, as the three leaders sped towards Bordeaux, one disaster after another was occurring behind them.

Barrow, driving a De Dietrich, swerved to avoid a dog and crashed into a tree. His mechanic was killed. Porter, in one of the Wolseley team cars, rounded a corner to find level-crossing gates closed against him. He turned off the road rather than crash through the gates, his car hit a house, burst into flames and again the mechanic died. Count de St James (Automotrice) went out after hitting a spectator's car, parked by the roadside. The American W.K. Vanderbilt Jnr retired and so did Baron de Forest (Mercedes).

Near Poitiers, disaster overtook Marcel Renault, brother of Louis. Marcel seemed to have a premonition before the race and had been strangely reluctant to start. He was driving flat out in pursuit of Théry (Decauville) and the cars reached a bend in close company. Neither driver would give way. Half-blinded by the dust rising in great storms from the wheels, Marcel forced his car past, inch by inch, but as he did so one wheel of the Renault hit the gutter at the side of the road, the car rolled over and over, smashing to smithereens and throwing out the helpless driver and mechanic.

Maurice Farman, who had been just behind the pair, pulled up and hurried to see what could be done but the crew of the Renault were dead. Théry drove on at a crawl, his nerve temporarily gone. Farman retired on the spot and so did the remaining Renault drivers as one by one they arrived at the scene of the accident.

Worse was to come. Tourand (Brouhot) saw a child in his path, wrenched at the wheel, lost control and skidded into the crowd, killing several people. All for nothing. The child he had tried to save died under the madly-spinning wheels of the giant car.

In Bordeaux, no one yet knew the sorry news and there were great cheers as Louis Renault sped into town, followed 15 minutes later by Jarrott.

Then nothing. . . .

The sun beat down on the milling throng, all sorts of rumours spread through the crowd but still no more cars came. . . .

Then, at long last, another car appeared at the end of the long straight tree-lined avenue and as it drew closer it was seen to carry the number '168'. What had happened to all the cars which had started before this one? As conjecture ran rampant, Fernand Gabriel brought his Mors into the control. He had passed more than 80 of his rivals as he burnt up the miles at a fantastic speed. But now others struggled in with tales of disaster. Someone brought the news of Marcel Renault's death. Louis retired from the race immediately and dashed back to the scene of the accident.

His retirement proved academic. The public outcry was so great that both French and Spanish governments intervened and ordered that the race be abandoned.

The Paris–Madrid was decided on the placings from Paris to Bordeaux. The bloody consequences obscured the magnificence of Gabriel's achievement for he was declared the winner, having covered 552 km (343 miles) at an average speed of 104.6 kph (65 mph). Louis Renault was placed second, having

Below: 1904 Gordon Bennett winner, Théry, is congratulated by the Kaiser. Bottom: Another of the historical Michelin tiles. This shows the great German driver, Lautenschlager (Mercedes), at full speed in the 1908 Automobile Club of France Grand Prix at Dieppe.

GRAND-PRIX de l'A·C·F· 1908 Dieppe LAUTENSCHLAGER sur MERCÉDÈS

averaged 99.8 kph (62 mph) in a car of 40-hp less than the winner, Salleron (Mors) was third and Jarrott fourth.

It was the end of an era in motor-racing, the virtual finish of town-to-town races on unguarded roads. With the exception of the Italian Mille Miglia, no race remotely comparable has since been held and the Mille Miglia itself came to a tragic end many years later when the Marquis de Portago was involved in a 1957-style version of the Paris–Madrid tragedy.

After the tragic events of 1903, motor races were held on specially constructed tracks or on roads closed to the public while the race was on. In England, Brooklands was opened in 1907 and two years later, in the USA, 'The Brickyard', otherwise known as the Indianapolis Speedway, came into being. Later came tracks at Montlhéry (France), Monza (Italy) and Avus (Germany).

But races were still organized before these tracks were opened. The Gordon Bennett Race was held again in 1904, this time in Germany, since that country had taken the honours in 1903. With Paris–Madrid in mind, many of the roads comprising the circuit were closed to all save the competitors, level-crossings were closed *against* the trains, and the racing cars were 'neutralized' when they passed through towns and villages. The sequel was a race which many regarded as the best of the series. It ended with Théry (Richard-Brasier) gaining the laurels for France, ahead of Jenatzy (Mercedes) and Rougier (Turcat-Méry). The leading British competitor, Girling (Wolseley), came ninth.

So it was back to France for 1905. By this time the motor-racing world was in a whirl. The British had decided to run a race of their own in the Isle of Man, the Tourist Trophy, today the oldest motor race in the world still being run and the French were at odds with every other motor racing nation. The main reason was that France proposed not only to run the Gordon Bennett but also to stage the world's first Grand Prix, in which the host nation would be permitted 16 entries against a maximim of 6 for any other country. To be fair to the French, there was something in their argument since no other nation had so many car manufacturers and it seemed unreasonable that they should be limited to the same representation as a nation which might have difficulty in scraping up three cars of any description. Eventually, the French achieved their ends. There was no Grand Prix in 1905 and the Gordon Bennett, in its dying throes, was won by Théry again, chased by two Italian FIATs with Rolls in a Wolseley finishing eighth. But, in 1906, came the Grand Prix.

Run in blazing heat over a distance of 1,239 km (770 miles) it took a tremendous toll of drivers, machines and tyres. Panhards produced an 18¼-litre monster especially for the race but, in the event, it was won by a more conventional 13-litre Renault. The car was French but the driver, Sziz, was Hungarian.

Few realized it at the time, but the Grand Prix was to become *the* major event in the motor-racing calendar. Meanwhile, the new specially designed close circuits attracted public attention.

In Britain, the prime mover was a man named Locke King who decided that the native motor industry needed a track where its products could be tested. At Weybridge, Surrey, with the enthusiastic co-operation of his wife, Locke King built Brooklands, a circuit which, Indianapolis apart, became probably the most famous in the world. At both circuits the spectator could see what was going on, something not always possible on modern circuits.

The first race meeting at Brooklands attracted about 14,000 spectators and there were some 500 cars in the official car-parks, a remarkable figure in 1907 when the total of cars registered throughout the British Isles was only 9,000.

The big race of the day was the Montagu Cup over a mere 48 kilometres (30 miles), but for the then considerable purse of £1,400. The entry list included some of the biggest and most powerful cars then in existence, driven by some of the leading drivers of the time. Best-known of them was Dario Resta who was to win the Vanderbilt Cup, the French Grand Prix and the Indianapolis 500 as a Peugeot driver. Here at Brooklands he drove a Mercedes. Another Mercedes was driven by J.E. Hutton. The favourite was Cecil Edge in his brother Selwyn's Napier.

Hutton's Mercedes made a good start but Edge, with a great burst of acceleration, caught the German car up and the wise ones concluded that the Napier was going to justify being favourite. They had a rude shock when Warwick Wright (Darracq) came up fast behind the two leaders and went to the front. After three laps Wright was still ahead with Edge in second place and the two Mercedes following, Resta being third and Hutton fourth.

A dramatic change of fortunes followed. Edge dropped out with fluid leaking from his car and Hutton overtook Resta to move into second place. Still Wright stayed in front, although his Darracq was, by the standard of the times, a veteran. The pace was proving too hot, however, and although Wright kept the lead through the fifth, sixth and seventh laps, trouble hit him the eighth time round and the car slowed down. On the ninth lap he pulled into the pits his race over: there was a hole in the crankshaft and a camshaft was bent. Hutton was also in trouble and down to three cylinders and so Resta swept into the lead.

Then came one of the sport's most tragic moments. As Resta approached the Fork for the last time, all over a winner, he saw, or thought he saw, a man waving him round again. Although he thought he was on the last lap, he obeyed the signal and continued for an extra circuit. Timekeeping being in its infancy and lap charts unheard of, it was assumed on the completion of his ninth lap that Resta had only just finished the race and so he was placed third, despite a protest. Hutton was declared the official winner with Okara's FIAT second. No official times were taken but the winner's speed was said to be around 132 kph (82 mph).

Hutton and Resta picked up a lot more prize money that season. Hutton won the £350 Heath Stakes and Resta and he finished first and second in the Prix de la France. In the first three meetings, the Mercedes cars earned £2,800, the Napiers £1,760 and the Darracqs £1,000. Translate that money into modern terms and it is obvious that the 'amateurs' and the 'chauffeurs' of motor-racing's early days did not do at all badly.

The Indianapolis Motor Speedway opened for business in August, 1909, when the barnstorming Barney Oldfield, driving a Benz, smashed five world records. But several accidents resulted in the deaths of three competitors and two spectators. It was obvious that the surface, not dissimilar to that of an ordinary road, was unsuitable for high-powered racing cars.

The track was closed and re-paved with bricks, a gold-plated brick being dropped into the last hole when the re-opening ceremony took place in December. Years afterwards the track was resurfaced again, this time with asphalt, leaving only a short stretch of brick. But the nickname, 'The Old Brickyard', remained.

Below: An advertising poster for the American Indianapolis Speedway, about 1910. Bottom: Fashionable spectators watch the 1906 French Grand Prix in what would today be regarded as very dangerous proximity to the racing cars.

On 30 May, 1911, the International Sweepstakes, the most important race in the circuit's short history, was held. Although none could have realized it at the time, it was to be the first in one of the most famous series of all motor-races, the classic Indianapolis 500 Miles Race.

The Sweepstakes had attracted no less than 40 entries, the cream of men and machines then in the USA. To some the race meant fortune or ruin. Harry Stutz, newcomer to the ranks of automobile manufacturers, was taking a gamble on an untried driver, Gil Anderson, whose previous racing experience had been as a riding mechanic with the Marmon Company. Another young manufacturer, Howard Marmon, was also taking a gamble. A brilliant designer but a not very good businessman, he was counting on Indianapolis to finally establish the name and reputation of his cars, of which he had entered two. One was to be driven by Joe Dawson, the other by a thin-faced, sparsely-thatched veteran named Ray Harroun, whom Marmon had persuaded out of a short-lived retirement.

Both Stutz and Marmon must have wondered how their entries would fare against star-studded opposition which included great drivers like the Italian-born Ralph DePalma; Bob Burman, winner of the first race ever held at the track; and 'Terrible Teddy' Tetzlaff, a rugged Westerner with a reputation for being both mean and mad behind the wheel. Tetzlaff and Mulford were driving for Lozier; Burman and Billy Knipper for Benz; Arthur Chevrolet and Charles Basle for Buick. There were three Fiats, piloted by David Bruce-Brown, Ed Hearne and Cal Bragg; and a lone Mercedes, driven by the millionaire sportsman, Spencer Wishart. Another fancied candidate was Louis Strang, who, after risking his neck so many times at 80 mph or more, was to die in a country lane when his car overturned at 4 mph.

A sudden hush fell on the eighty thousand people watching as the cars lined up in ranks of five, one hundred feet between each group. At the head, to act as pacemaker, was a roadster supplied by the Stoddard Company of Dayton, Ohio, an enterprising firm which once had one of their cars hoisted into the air by a balloon as a publicity stunt. The pacemaker was being driven by one of the founders of the Indianapolis, Carl G. Fisher, and he it was who now gave the word of command to move off.

The thunder of engines broke the silence, the cars speeded up to 64.4 kph (40 mph) and, as they came into the straight, closed formation and roared away, the roadster pulling off the track. The starting-bomb signalled that the race was under way.

Aitken shot into the lead, but his National stayed in front for only a few laps before succumbing to the challenge of Wishart in the Mercedes. This car, reputedly the most expensive in the race, having, it was said, cost its owner-driver some $63,000, kept the lead although hard-pressed by Fred Belcher (Knox) and David Bruce-Brown.

Belcher was surprising the pundits by his showing. He clung grimly to the tail of the Mercedes and Wishart's concentration began to waver under the unrelenting pursuit. A moment of uncertainty and Belcher swept past him – but not for long. Almost immediately Bruce-Brown took over the lead. Belcher, however, was keeping in touch, Aitken was there or thereabouts and Ralph DePalma had moved up into the leading bunch.

Behind the leaders, much was happening. Harroun, going well in the leading Marmon, a car nicknamed the *Wasp* because of its narrow body and pointed tail, had pulled into the pits and handed over to his relief driver, Cyrus Patschke, rather to everyone's surprise. Patschke, however, drove with unsuspected panache to keep contact with the leaders. A hundred miles later he handed back to Harroun with the Marmon very well-placed indeed and the strategy, if strategy it was, began to pay off handsomely.

Harroun now produced some touches bordering on genius, overtaking rival after rival. Most of the cars carried riding mechanics who warned their drivers of other cars coming up astern. The narrow cockpit of the Marmon had room only for the driver, so Harroun relied on a rear-view mirror, a device which was, of course, to become a standard fitment on all cars. Harroun's mirror on this occasion was not over-worked since he was doing most of the overtaking.

By now the leaders had covered nearly half the distance, not without incident but certainly without serious trouble, although there was a scare when oil bathed the track at the first turn and had to be hastily sanded by officials. It was too happy a state of affairs to last. One of the Case cars, driven by Joe Jagersberger, was just pulling out of the pits when a steering-knuckle broke. The sudden swerve threw out Anderson, the riding mechanic, and spectators gasped with horror as they saw his prostrate figure lying on the track. Meanwhile, the Case, completely out of control, gyrated crazily across the track and smashed into the judges' stand.

Anderson lay where he had fallen, right in the path of another car, a Westcott driven by Harry Knight, which was now thundering down upon him. Knight desperately wrenched his steering wheel to the left in a bid to avoid the mechanic and crashed full tilt into Herb Lytle's Apperson which was standing in the pits undergoing tyre changes. The Apperson was hurled bodily into the air and into the Benz pit, narrowly missing the four occupants. The Westcott turned over and over, finally coming to rest against a Fiat which was also stationary in the pits. So great was the force of the collision that the entire pit structure swayed and bent. Knight and his mechanic, Glover, were thrown about 25 feet through the air and both were taken to hospital, Knight with a suspected skull fracture and Glover with a strained back and internal injuries. Miraculously they were the only two serious casualties.

Positions were now changing so fast that the scoreboard gave up the unequal struggle to keep spectators informed. Bruce-Brown, at one time in the lead by about 12.9 km (8 miles), lost his advantage to Aitken and DePalma when he pitted, but he was soon back in front again. With attention divided between the leaders and the dramatic happenings in the pits few people took much notice of the sleek *Wasp* edging its way through the field. So Bruce-Brown, concentrating grimly, was startled when his mechanic tapped him on the shoulder to warn that a car was coming up.

It was Harroun and the Marmon and nothing Bruce-Brown could do prevented the unsmiling veteran going ahead. But there was little in it. Wishart, DePalma, Charlie Merz at the wheel of a National, and Harroun's own team-mate, Joe Dawson, were all still in with a chance.

Could any of them catch the speeding *Wasp*? It seemed doubtful. Harroun was cornering with practised ease and his car seemed to have too many 'horses' for the others down the straights. Ralph Mulford had other ideas. His team-mate, 'Terrible Teddy', was out of the running but now Mulford, a Sunday School teacher who always wore a starched white collar even when racing, began driving like the Devil himself, turning in laps of more than 128.7 kph (80 mph).

The pace was a hot one. Too hot. Disaster struck again. An Amplex with Art Greiner at the wheel was going into a bend when both rear tyres burst

simultaneously. Dickson, the mechanic, was thrown against the fence and killed instantly. Greiner was more fortunate, crawling from the wreckage nursing a broken arm. The pace told too on Mulford's tyres and any chance he had of catching Harroun disappeared with slow work in the Lozier pits, seconds being wasted on every stop.

Harroun, sensing victory was his, let the *Wasp* full out for the last few laps, roaring over the finishing-line nearly two minutes ahead of Mulford, whose gallant efforts had been frustrated by the fumbling fingers of his mechanics. Harroun, with the aid of Patschke, had driven a masterly race, covering the 500 miles in 6 hrs 42 mins 8 secs, at an average speed of 119 kph (74 mph), to win $10,000.

After Mulford, but some way behind, came Bruce-Brown's Fiat, Wishart's Mercedes and Dawson's Marmon. DePalma was sixth, Merz seventh, Turner (Amplex) eighth, Belcher ninth and Cobe (Jackson) tenth. Out of the prize-money, but making a promising start to an illustrious racing career, was Gil Anderson, who brought the Stutz home eleventh.

Harroun went back into retirement and this time stayed there. Marmon continued to manufacture cars until 1933, when the firm was finally forced to give up the struggle against the giants of the industry. Harroun's driving-mirror was just one of the innovations which gained the spotlight at Indianapolis. Four-wheel brakes, straight-eight motors, balloon tyres and ethyl gasoline were others, although historians disagree on credits for these developments, as they do on most innovations in the motor industry.

One thing was certain; Brooklands and Indianapolis had introduced types of racing which were to survive for many, many years – in the case of Indianapolis until the present.

The world's first motor-racing track as distinct from road racing circuits, was Brooklands, near Weybridge, Surrey, England.

The Manufacturers

As far as the USA and the majority of the motor manufacturing nations of Europe are concerned, the industry has had three main phases: the early years when every inventor, blacksmith, machinist and entrepreneur turned his attention to manufacturing or marketing cars – the list of American manufacturers alone ran into thousands; between the wars when competition was cut-throat, the number of manufacturing companies dwindled and many smaller ones went to the wall; and the post-Second World War period when, insofar as generalizations are ever correct, just a few dominant manufacturers, sometimes complemented by a handful of specialist builders, commanded the market in each country.

The German and French industries led the way, the Americans came swiftly into the picture, the Italian and British manufacturers followed and flourished – a situation which maintained itself throughout most of the twentieth century. Few of the smaller European nations, e.g. Holland, Belgium, Austria, etc., became leaders in the industry; even fewer of the Eastern European countries, including Russia, made a real impact. It was not until after the Second World War that another major factor came into the picture with the burgeoning Japanese industry.

The angle at which this photograph is taken makes the 1902 Mercedes, a racing car with a distinguished record, appear more squat than it was in fact.

Perhaps the easiest way to study the evolution of the motor car industry is to take the story, nation by nation, from the earliest cars to the present day. And since it seems unanswerable that Karl Benz was the first of the early 'inventors' to manufacture cars for general sale to the public, it seems reasonable to start with . . .

Below: A 25/35 horse-power Panhard Landaulette.
Bottom: In vivid contrast, a 1957 Mercedes-Benz 300 SL, another car with a distinguished sporting record. It was known as the 'Gull-wing' because the side windows and roof looked like wings when they were raised for driver and passenger to get in.

25/35 H.P. PANHARD-LEVASSOR LANDAULETTE.

Germany

The industry founded by Benz expanded and prospered, but Benz himself refused to accept the giant strides made by others, notably his fellow-countrymen Daimler and Maybach, and recognized only the minor modifications he himself made. The result was that although the Benz firm was pre-eminent in the early days of car manufacture, its sales dwindled and dropped after the turn of the century and, eventually, after the First World War, Benz were amalgamated with Daimler to form the giant Mercedes-Benz organization. Thus Daimler and Benz who, for some reason, never met in life, were united in death. Karl Benz died at Ladenburg on 4 April, 1929, undoubtedly the true father of the automobile.

Gottlieb Daimler may have come after Benz in the founding of the industry, but he certainly outstripped him in moving with the times. Notably, Daimler realized that the future of the automobile lay with the light, high-speed engine rather than the slow, heavy, stationary-type engine with which Benz persevered. In one respect Daimler lagged behind: he persevered with hot-tube ignition when even Benz used electric.

If Benz was the industry's founding father, Daimler paved the way for it in other countries by licensing his patents to people like Sarazin in France and Harry Lawson and Frederick Simms in Great Britain. In particular, the Sarazin deal, which involved the Panhard et Levassor company, led to a great step

forward in the development of the motor car.

When Daimler died in 1900, the firm was carried on by his partner and collaborator, Wilhelm Maybach, who brought in still more improvements, including a pressed-steel chassis, gate gear-change and honeycomb radiator. Maybach was persuaded by one Emil Jellinek that there was considerable sales resistance in France to the Teutonic Daimler name (the Franco-Prussian War had not been forgotten) and so Mercedes came into being, named after Jellinek's daughter. As Mercedes, the products of Daimler continued to flourish and develop, to such an extent that, as early as 1922, a car with a supercharger was marketed.

Over the years more great names were to appear on the German motoring scene, among them Opel, BMW, Porsche, Auto-Union, NSU, Messerschmidt and others. But, as in other countries, various mergers took place. Opel became the German arm of the giant American General Motors; another American giant, Ford, opened a German plant. Audi swallowed up NSU and in turn were swallowed up themselves; a familiar pattern in all car-making countries. But, after Daimler and Benz, the true German success story is 'The People's Car'.

The best-selling Volkswagen, the *Beetle* as it was nicknamed, fitted the purse and captured the imagination, not only of the Germans, but others in war-torn Europe. It became a popular car all over the world and by the time production ceased in 1978, it had provided one of the great stories of motoring history, rivalling that of Henry Ford's Model T.

At the time of going to press, the leading German manufacturers, in order of cars produced per annum, were: VW 1,208,867; Opel (General Motors) 922,304; Ford 542,750; Daimler Benz 409,090; Audi NSU (Volkswagen) 317,928; BMW 284,771.

France

If it was the Germans who founded the car industry, it was the French who improved upon it and expanded it.

It began with a man named Sarazin to whom Daimler allocated the French rights to his patents. Sarazin commissioned a friend, Emile Levassor, who was in partnership with René Panhard in a woodworking business, to build him a petrol-engine. Before it was completed Sarazin died. Daimler, impressed by his widow's business acumen, reallocated the rights to her. Levassor, presumably impressed by the lady's charms, married her. And so Panhard et Levassor went into the car manufacturing business.

At the time, most cars consisted of a horse-carriage with an engine installed in a convenient place, usually over the rear axle. Levassor constructed something we would recognize as a car and installed the engine in front. This first Panhard et Levassor was a model for most of the motor cars to come. Panhards enjoyed an enviable reputation over the years, especially for better-class touring cars and it was well after the Second World War before they dropped out of the limelight.

Another famous French manufacturer, Peugeot,

evolved from friendship with Levassor. Armand Peugeot, sent to England by the family firm of Peugeot Frères, manufacturing ironmongers, for his engineering and commercial training, became interested in bicycles. With ironmongery agents all over France, the Peugeot cycles were soon selling well.

Peugeot and Levassor did business over woodworking machinery and Levassor tried to persuade Armand of the great future for self-propelled carriages. Peugeot, half-convinced, was not sure about petrol-engines and eventually signed an agreement with Serpollet, the steam car builder. The Peugeot-Serpollet was not a success, however, and Peugeot went back to Levassor for petrol-engines. The Peugeot-Levassor was a success, so much so that after

1896 Peugeot built their own engines. One of the most famous of their early cars was the Baby Peugeot.

Louis Renault built his first car in 1898. It was basically the bits and pieces from a De Dion tricycle, particularly the engine, with pneumatic tyres and wheel steering added. His brothers, Marcel and Fernand, joined him, they achieved considerable racing success and another French automobile giant was on the way. An offshoot, the British Renault company was formed in 1902. Renault, now state-owned, remains a key organization in the manufacture of modern cars.

Bollée, which played a very important part in the first years of the motor car, did not long survive the First World War and eventually the works were purchased by William Morris, later Lord Nuffield, one of the British motor tycoons.

There were many other famous French cars between the wars but the majority do not survive today. Darracq (who merged with Talbot in 1919), Delage, Delahaye, De Dion Bouton (prolific manufacturers in the first few years as shown by the number of such cars which take part in Britain's annual London to Brighton Run), Decauville, Charron, CVG, Chenard et Walcker (great Le Mans cars in the early days of the

Bottom: This might be termed the French 'People's Car'. The Citroen 2CV, in its various forms, is a car ranking with the VW, the Model T Ford, the Austin Seven and other great popular cars. Inset: A 1900 De Dion Bouton.

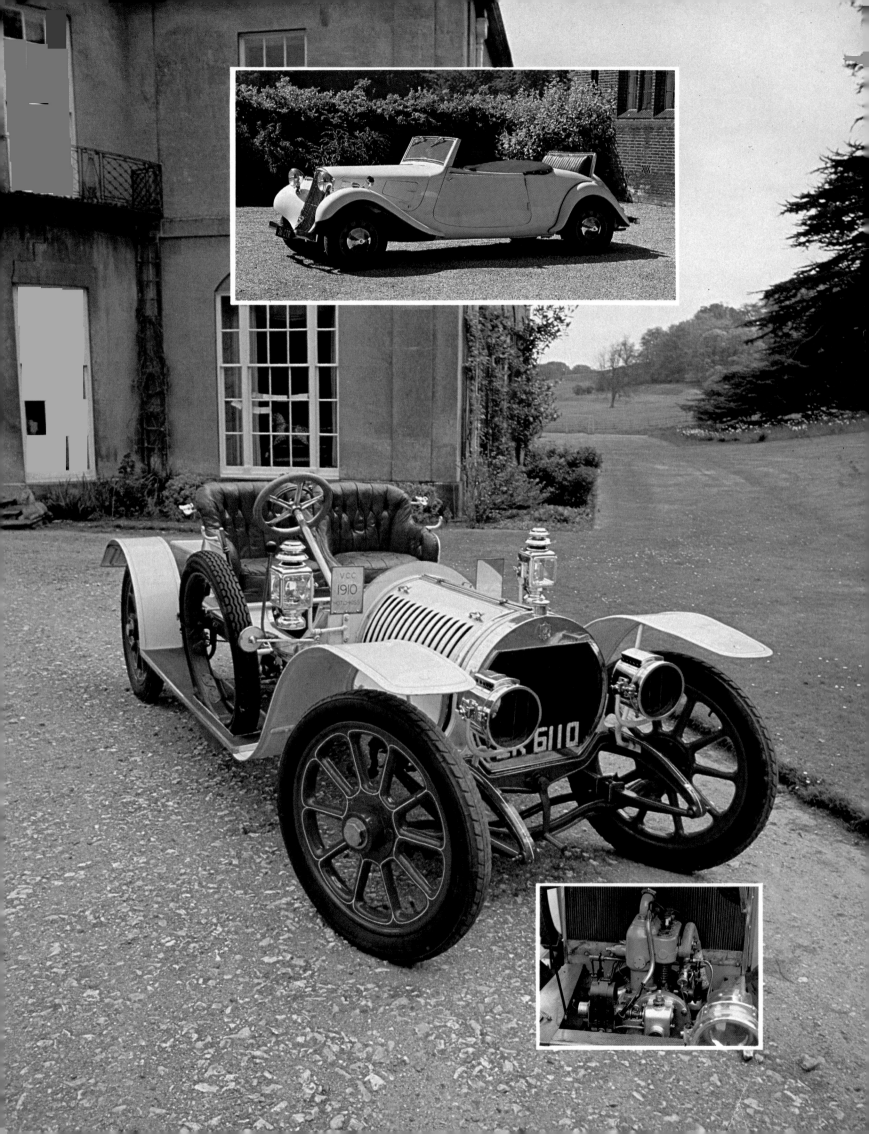

event), Hotchkiss (a company founded by an American in Paris) and all the varieties of Talbot, Clement-Talbot, Clement-Bayard and so on. Plus, of course, the great Bugattis, whose fame is largely due to extraordinary exploits on the race circuits of the world.

One name which has survived, however, to stand alongside Renault and Peugeot, is Citroën. As far back as 1919, Citroën introduced tough little utility cars, good on economy if not performance and able, as one writer commented, 'to stand the iniquities inflicted on them by French drivers'. It is for this type of car, of which the 2CV is a modern version, that Citroën are most famous, although they have also produced more powerful and luxurious cars such as the post-Second World War Safari. In many respects, the smaller Citroëns deserve to rank alongside the Volkswagen in Germany, the Baby Austin and later the Mini in Britain and the Model T Ford in the States.

Even the French have been unable to resist amalgamation and rationalization in their car industry. There are now two giant concerns, Renault and PSA Peugeot Citroën who, at the time of going to press, are in the process of taking over Chrysler's UK operation. Peugeot produce 676,109 cars in a year and Citroën 607,280, giving the combine an annual production of 1,283,389. Renault just top this if the output of their Spanish subsidiary is included in their total.

Right, inset top: A 1936 Citroën Traction Avant Convertible. Inset bottom: The engine of a 1909 Renault. The main picture shows the beautiful 1910 Hotchkiss. Below: One of motoring's more elegant marques, the Hispano-Suiza. The car shown is a 1912 model.

French production is completed by the American firm of Chrysler, which took over Simca. They now build 475,565 cars a year.

Spain

Today, the Spanish industry is largely influenced from France, Italy and the United States. In the past there were Spanish cars of some renown, notably the Hispano-Suiza, designed by a Swiss and built in both Spain and France and one of the classic cars of all time.

Today, SEAT is the nearest to a truly Spanish car, although the company is part-owned by the Italian Fiat concern and the SEAT cars are very closely based upon Fiat designs. In 1977, SEAT built 346,535 cars but sales have suffered since Ford launched the Fiesta in Spain (Ford sales 213,268) and the drive of Fasa Renault, the Spanish subsidiary of the giant French state-controlled company (sales 224,358). Chrysler also have a Spanish subsidiary (sales 96,435).

Great Britain

As in a number of countries today, the British car industry consists of a few very large firms plus a handful of specialist manufacturers. There is the giant BL (British Leyland) concern which, over the years and under different names, has swallowed up Austin, Morris, Wolseley, Standard-Triumph, MG, Jaguar, Riley and Rover; two American-owned companies, Vauxhall (part of the General Motors group) and Ford; and a third American-owned company (the former Rootes group) Chrysler which, as this book went to press, was about to be taken over by the French Peugeot-Citroën combine. And there is the unique Rolls-Royce company.

The most important companies after this are
Reliant, who make three-wheelers as well as the more
exciting Scimitar; and Lotus who, apart from fame on
the race tracks, make fast sports cars. There are a
handful of others, amongst which Aston-Martin, with
very de luxe models indeed, is the best-known.

Britain, like the USA, at first had hundreds of
manufacturers, but many had expired by the time the
First World War started and others were either
swallowed up by larger companies between the wars
or else went broke.

In the pioneer manufacturing period, the
Lanchester brothers, led by Dr Frederick Lanchester,
were pre-eminent. Lanchester cars were far ahead of
their time. Amongst Lanchester's many inventions
was an early form of disc brake. But like so many
brilliant men, his business acumen did not match his
other qualities and Lanchester faded from the scene as
an independent manufacturer.

The two giants among British manufacturers were
Herbert (later Lord) Austin and William Morris (later
Lord Nuffield). Austin, a first-class designer in his
own right, worked first on Wolseleys before setting up
his Austin company, the most famous creation of
which was the Austin Seven, or 'Baby Austin'. But
Austins also made saloon cars of every type, plus a
number of useful racers and record-breakers during
the Brooklands era.

Starting with a cycle shop in Oxford and an acute
business brain, Morris successfully built up his
company. These two concerns dominated the British
market for years and it was their eventual merger
which led to the formation of what is now BL.

Vauxhall and Rootes were the other two major
pioneering concerns which have carried on until
present times, although Vauxhall were taken over by
General Motors in 1925, and Rootes later became the
British end of the American Chrysler operation, after
themselves taking in such companies as Humber,
Hillman and Singer.

To the rest of the world, Rolls-Royce, founded by a
dashing scion of the aristocracy and a dour Northern
engineer, epitomize the British car. They are still the
outstanding prestige symbol, the embodiment of all
that is luxurious.

Jaguar and Rover, although now part of the BL
empire, are also worth mentioning.

Jaguar, the brain-child of a sidecar manufacturer
named William Lyons (who was later knighted),
became the world's outstanding sports car. For years
the cars dominated Le Mans and also provided an
integral part of the post-Second World War sports-
car scene in the USA.

Rover, although also noted for quality saloon cars,
have a niche in motoring history for developing that
highly-successful utility vehicle, the Land-Rover
(British equivalent of the American Jeep), and its
more sophisticated cousin, the Range Rover.

Sadly, many other British manufacturers who
produced quantities of cars in their time – Daimler,
BSA, Bentley, Lea-Francis, Crossley, Straker-
Squire, Sunbeam, etc. – are now just names in the
record-books.

In the mass markets of the world, British Leyland is
a middling-size company with 1977 sales of 651,069.

Elegance in every line: a 1931 Rolls-Royce Phantom II Continental and (inset) an R series Bentley Continental two-door fastback.

Ford of Britain's figure was 406,633, Chrysler's 169,492, and Vauxhall's (General Motors) 93,237.

Then comes Reliant, Rolls-Royce, Lotus, TVR and Panther, the newest company of all, which produces cars on classic lines.

Aston-Martin, now combined with Lagonda, and AC are two great names of the past still in business, but their cars are produced in comparatively tiny numbers. And the little Morgan Company soldiers on, selling all it can make of the sporty cars which have not changed much in appearance since the thirties.

Italy

It may just be the Italian language, but the names of Italian car manufacturers always seem to have a romantic ring, starting with one of the oldest, Isotta Fraschini (1899) and continuing through such as Lancia, Alfa-Romeo, Maserati, Ferrari and Lamborghini. Alfas are very much still in business, but throughout the century the dominant Italian manufacturer has been Fiat.

Founded by a young cavalry officer named Giovanni Agnelli, in association with a group of wealthy aristocrats, Fiat cars were originally marketed as FIAT: Fabrica Italiana Automobili Torino. Today, with an Agnelli still at the helm, Fiat is one of the key firms in Italian industry and one of the world's most important car manufacturers.

Key men in the early development were two brilliant designers, Aristide Faccioli and Giovanni Enrico, and two great racing drivers, Vincenzo Lancia and Felice Nazzaro, both of whom went on to become manufacturers themselves, Lancia rather more successfully than Nazzaro.

Founded, like Isotta, in 1899, Fiat produced less than 200 vehicles in 1901. By 1977, however, that figure had grown to 1,200,707, not counting the Fiat-

Above: The award-winning Range Rover, a successor of that famous utility vehicle, the Land Rover. Below: A Japanese car which surprised many people, including the rallying world, the 1972 Datsun 240Z.

based vehicles produced by SEAT in Spain and the Polski-Fiats of Poland. In contrast, the only other major Italian manufacturer of today, Alfa-Romeo, produced 201,118 units in 1977.

Fiat construction has not been confined to motor cars. Aeroplanes, armoured cars, tractors, tanks, buses, coaches, powerboats, railway trains . . . have all poured from the factories of what is probably the most important industrial firm in Italy.

Two things have marked the progress of both Fiat and Alfa-Romeo. They have always produced attractive designs, giving rise to the tag 'Every Italian engineer is an artist at heart', and they have always raced. Indeed, it is the proud boast of Alfas that they have been racing – *and winning* – all over the world for more than 60 years. Amongst their successes they claim 5 World Championships, 11 Mille Miglia races, 10 Targa Florios, 4 Le Mans 24 Hours, and over 100 Grand Prix races. And for good measure they also claim 149 speedboat championships in the last 10 years.

Japan

The Japanese make no claims to have invented the automobile, but if they were not in at the beginning of the motor industry they have certainly made up for it since.

Today the Japanese auto industry produces some 8 million or so vehicles annually, of which more than 5 million are passenger vehicles.

The Toyota firm ranks behind only the American General Motors and Ford companies, although Nissan has become another strong Japanese contender. Toyota are responsible for the most popular Japanese model, the Corolla, production of which has reached as high as three-quarters of a million in one year. Other big sellers in recent years have been the Nissan Sunny and the Honda Civic.

Toyo Kogyo and Mitsubishi are close behind Honda in passenger car production and Fuji are also in business in a big way. Fuji Heavy Industries, founded in 1917 as the Nakajima aircraft organization, today numbers among its many products the Subaru range of motor cars, voted, in 1975, the USA's Import Car of the Year.

Isuzu, Daihatsu and Suzuki complete the list of passenger car builders, although there are other manufacturers building only commercial vehicles.

Japan is responsible for more than 20 per cent of all the cars produced in the world. Something like 4 million vehicles are exported each year but their products are often more familiar in other countries under names like Datsun (Nissan), Mazda (Toyo Kogyo) and Colt (Mitsubishi). In fact, Japanese car nomenclature can be very confusing to those accustomed to Western methods. For example, the 1979 Mazda was named *Montrose* for the UK market, *the 626* for other export markets and *Capella* in Japan itself.

Australia

Australia was early in the field of motor car manufacture, although Blackburn's early mechanical vehicle, described in chapter 1, appears to have been a 'one-off'.

In 1897, the Australian Horseless Carriage Syndicate was formed and the following year the Pioneer car made its appearance. A four-seater running on kerosene, it was said to be capable of 10 mph. The body was built by a man named Jackson and the engine by a man named Grayson, both of Melbourne. It is believed that quite a number of these cars were manufactured.

Meanwhile, the Tarrant Company of Melbourne, manufacturers of oil and gas engines, also turned their thoughts to cars and the first Tarrant, designed by Colonel Harley Tarrant, appeared in 1900. By 1902 they were producing a 4-cylinder car fitted with solid tyres and in 1904/5 built what they described as a 'standard' car, one that could be supplied with either a 2- or 4-cylinder engine. These cars remained in production until 1907.

However, the ubiquitous American Ford Company had reached across the Pacific and the Ford S Roadster was selling in Australia for less than the Tarrant 2-cylinder.

Being realists, Tarrants gave up production themselves and acquired the Ford agency for Australia. This set the pattern for the motor industry in Australia which, henceforth, was largely to be American-dominated with a large number of imports especially, in modern times, from Japan.

Fords retained their early connections with Australia and subsequently set up their own plants there. The Ford Australian product best-known in Europe is the Fairmont.

General Motors moved into Australia in 1926 and in 1948 introduced the first mass-produced car to be manufactured in that country, the Holden. It remains the best-known Australian car, both inside and outside the country of its origin.

USA

The story of auto manufacture in the United States of America would fill a thousand-volume library but, in essence, it is dominated by two companies, General Motors and Ford.

Today, the giant General Motors has 121 plants operating in 21 states and 77 cities in the United States; 7 plants in Canada; and assembly, manufacturing, distribution and warehousing facilities in no less than 33 other countries.

It began like this. . . .

In 1897, R.E. Olds built his first successful Oldsmobile. Five years later H.M. Leland founded Cadillac and in 1903 the Buick Motor Company was formed from an earlier firm established by David Buick. In 1907, E.M. Murphy founded the Oakland Motor Company in Pontiac, Michigan. These four firms became the nucleus of General Motors, following its incorporation by W.C. Durant on 16 September, 1908.

Durant was a creator and salesman but not a good administrator, and the concern had anxious times before Alfred P. Sloan Jnr assumed the presidency in 1923. The firm realized the folly of relying entirely on outside agencies for parts and so they took over various parts and accessory manufacturers, including the Champion Ignition Company (now AC Spark Plug Division).

Chevrolet cars were taken over in 1918; Vauxhall Motors of England in 1925; and Adam Opel of Germany in 1929. Manufacturing began in Australia in 1948 (General Motors had been assembling cars there since 1926) and factories were set up later in Argentina, Brasil, Mexico and South Africa.

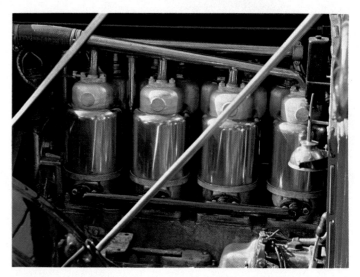

Left: A 1903 Oldsmobile, the 'popular' car of its time. Many are still running in veteran and antique car events. Above: The engine of a 1913 Cadillac. Opposite: A great name in the American luxury car market, the Packard. This is a 1940 model.

Among the significant General Motors developments which have influenced the car industry are:

1908: Britain's Royal Automobile Club awarded the Dewar Trophy to Cadillac for demonstrating the interchangeability of parts. Three Cadillacs were taken to pieces, the parts mixed up and the cars reassembled.

1910: Cadillac became the first manufacturer to offer closed bodies as standard equipment.

1911: First successful electric self-starter devised by C.F. Kettering and used by Cadillac.

1923: Four-wheel brakes appeared on 1924 Buicks.

1926: Pontiac car introduced by Oakland.

Cadillac introduced shatter-resistant safety glass.

1928: Synchromesh transmission introduced by Cadillac.

1933: Individual front-wheel suspension developed by GM.

1939: First completely automatic transmission introduced on 1940 Oldsmobiles.

1940: General Motors produced its 25 millionth car.

1952: Power steering offered by Cadillac, Oldsmobile and Buick.

1953: Power brakes offered by Buick and Oldsmobile.

1954: General Motors produced its 50 millionth US-made car.

1962: General Motors produced its 75 millionth car made in US.

1966: Energy-absorbing steering column introduced.

1967: General Motors produced its 100 millionth US-made car.

Wherever General Motors went, they were followed by Ford – and very often found that Ford had

got there first.

The great success of the Model T, 'the car that put the world on wheels', has tended to obscure the fact that Fords introduced many other remarkable cars. One of these was the 933 cc Model Y, the company's first venture into the 8-hp field. In spite of its incredibly low price (the price of the fully-equipped car was progressively reduced until it sold for £100), the car was nevertheless an attractive, reliable, comfortable, serious vehicle in every way; well appointed and equipped and with a performance of 99.76 kph (62 mph) maximum speed; 0–80.45 kph (0–50 mph) in 34 seconds. Model Y was produced between 1932 and 1937. It weighed only 14 cwt and consequently 40 mpg could be obtained on normal driving. With all these qualities, the car was aptly-called the 'Popular' from 1935. Two other Fords with a great impact on the British market were the post-war Anglia 105E and the Cortina, which began production in 1962 and was still going strong, albeit with modifications, in 1978.

In the United States the very powerful Mustangs helped the sporty image Ford have always cultivated; and the small Fiesta, originated in Spain, indicated the company's willingness to seek means of meeting the requirements of international markets.

Also alive and kicking in the United States is American Motors. Although not too successful in overseas marketing, the company, in 1978, was negotiating with the state-owned French Renault company a deal which would not only make AM's distribution network in the USA available to the French, but would also permit the manufacture of some Renault models.

Mention must also be made of some of the other great cars produced in the USA. For instance, 'The Three P's', cars which when the industry was in its

Among the illustrious early motor cars which, alas, are no more were the Pierce-Arrow and the Peerless (insets). The 1916 Mercer Tourer, as shown in the main illustration, was a car which many would like to own today.

infancy fought their ways to strong positions in the quality car field – Packard, Peerless and Pierce-Arrow. Packard, based in Detroit, first appeared in 1899; Peerless, based in Cleveland, followed a year later; and Pierce-Arrow emerged in Buffalo in 1901.

For more than 20 years, Packard was the Rolls-Royce of America, a car of quality, usually owned by people of means. The Depression of 1929 killed all that, and as the demand for luxury cars dropped so did Packard sales. Facing the inevitable, Packard moved into the mass market while still manufacturing luxury cars for those fortunate enough to be able to buy them.

Barney Oldfield, who did so much to boost the prestige of Ford on the race tracks, also played a significant part in the rise of Peerless. Driving the *Green Dragon*, he won race after race and broke record after record until in 1905 at St Louis he demolished a fence and two spectators, broke a few ribs and pierced a lung. Peerless built *Green Dragon* No. 2 and Oldfield drove it successfully until 1908. Peerless disappeared in 1932, following the Depression, but in the intervening years, the cars and their brilliant designer, Louis Mooers, played an important role in the development of the modern automobile.

George N. Pierce was a bird-cage and bicycle manufacturer when he built his first car, the Motorette, in 1901. It was powered by a De Dion engine. The first Arrow was introduced in 1903. The make became established when George's son, Percy P. Pierce, driving a Great Arrow, won the 1905 1,384 km (860 mile) Glidden Tour with 996 out of 1,000 points.

In later years, the cars were to set many records on the Utah Salt Flats, but Pierce-Arrow also suffered the aftermath of the Depression and the firm expired early in 1938.

One other car must be mentioned. The mighty Mercer company flourished in Trenton, New Jersey, from 1909 to 1925 building passenger touring cars and limousines of excellent mechanical quality. But the car which made their name was the Raceabout, a two-seater manufactured between 1910 and 1915.

It is ironic for the makers of cars like the Pierce-Arrow and the Peerless that American manufacturers are moving more and more into the luxury market, the market which disappeared in the thirties and left so many firms facing bankruptcy. But luxury market, or not, in 1977, the USA produced 9,213,600 cars and that represented a 9.4 per cent increase over the previous year.

Canada

With the giant American automotive empire just across the border, it is not surprising that the industry in Canada is very American-influenced.

The story is somewhat similar to the Australian experience.

In 1907 the McLaughlin Motor Car Company

Limited began manufacturing Buicks under contract, and participated in organizing the Chevrolet Motor Company of Canada in 1915. The two firms were merged to form General Motors of Canada Limited in 1918. There are now six manufacturing centres in five cities in Ontario and one in the Province of Quebec, with the headquarters of GM's Canadian operation in Oshawa, Ontario.

Sweden

Saab-Scania and Volvo are the famous names of the Swedish car industry. The former is old enough to have cars eligible for the Brighton Run, the event for cars manufactured before 1905.

Both firms have made a reputation on the sporting scene but through rallying rather than racing. Saab, in particular, with Erik Carlsson, had some wonderful victories in the 1960s in the Monte Carlo and RAC International Rallies.

Volvo lead the way today (production in 1977 171,800) with SAAB showing figures for the same year of 76,498.

Volvo also moved into the Netherlands, taking over the DAF firm, and the company has been further strengthened by a financial transfusion from the Norwegian government

Holland and Belgium

Both countries had famous makes in the early days of the motor car but, alas, have since fallen on hard times from a manufacturing point of view.

Dechamps was one of the earliest Belgian firms, first making tricycles and then conventional cars. Minerva was another make to last a good many years, while Metallurgique might have gone on to great things had it not been for the First World War. The company was originally a manufacturer of railway locomotives and rolling stock and went into car production as early as 1898. The cars did well in races, sold successfully in Britain and were manufactured under licence in Germany. But the Germans stripped the works during the war and although the company resumed production afterwards, Metallurgique never regained their pre-war eminence.

Vivinus, Pieper and the Miesse Steamer were other early Belgian efforts.

Today, the leading 'Belgian' manufacturer has the familiar name of Ford and, in 1977, produced 305,589 cars.

The Netherlands, too, was well-served in the pioneering days, with great cars like the Spyker which featured in the classic veteran car film *Genevieve*. Then, in modern times, the DAF, a car with a unique pulley transmission system, was prominent for a while until taken over by the Swedish Volvo firm. The new company, Volvo Car BV produced only 54,000 cars in 1977.

Eastern Europe

The countries of Eastern Europe have tended to produce cars more notable for solid reliability than for elegance and speed. It is a generalization which applies certainly to the Russian Moskvich and Lada cars, to the East German Wartburgs and to most of the Czech Skodas.

Not that reliability need be sneezed at – the Wartburg and Skoda teams have given many fine performances in one of the world's toughest rallies, the RAC International.

Lada are currently selling very well in the United Kingdom followed by Skoda and Polski-Fiat with Wartburg trailing badly, partly due to present-day construction restrictions on fuel emission.

The Czech Skodas have a long tradition: the original Laurin and Klement firm started making motor-cycles in 1899 and produced its first car in 1905; but manufacture is concentrated on cars which are economical both to buy and run. One way in which the Czechs achieve this is by not making drastic changes to models each year, preserving continuity much as VW did with the Beetle.

Possibly the Iron Curtain country to watch most closely is Poland. The Polski-Fiat, based upon the Fiat 125P, has been a success and now the Poles are developing their own cars, the Polonez making its debut in 1979. This car, a five-door hatchback, represents the first move by an Eastern bloc manufacturer to emulate Western design trends. Selling in Britain, for example, at under £3,000, the Polish car may well make an impression on the market.

So the industry grows and develops – South Korea now has a flourishing car factory, Turkey, Israel and other countries are joining the flow . . . selling cars looks likely to be a highly competitive market for many years to come.

A sturdy Swedish car which had a name for reliability and did well in rallies, the 1946 Volvo 444.

Racing Between the Wars

In 1936, Tazio Nuvolari, arguably the greatest racing-driver the world has ever known, went to the USA to take part in a revival of one of the oldest of motoring events, the Vanderbilt Cup. This had been instituted in 1904 by W.K. Vanderbilt Jnr, an American millionaire, who was a motor-racing enthusiast. In 1904 he put up the cash and trophies for the Vanderbilt Cup, a race to be run in Long Island, USA, but open to cars from Europe as well as the States. He stipulated that the cars, lock, stock and tyres, had to be made in the vehicle's country of origin. There was also an upper weight limit of 2,204 pounds.

That very first Vanderbilt Cup was won by George Heath (Panhard) at a speed of 83.99 kph (52.2 mph)

with Albert Clement (Clement-Bayard) second and Herb Lytle (Pope-Toledo) third. The series continued until 1916 when it foundered upon the entry of the USA into the First World War.

Then, 20 years later, the race was revived, this time under the benevolent eye of another millionaire, George, nephew of founder William, and still on Long Island, but at a new venue, the Roosevelt Raceway.

Europe's crack drivers were invited to compete against the best that America could offer. From Italy,

Left: Front cover of the programme for the 1936 Monaco Grand Prix. Below: One of the British Bentleys which dominated Le Mans in the twenties and thirties. Bugatti called them 'the fastest lorries in the world'. Overleaf: The famous Le Mans crash at White House Corner, a painting by F. Gordon Crosby.

The 1938/9 Mercedes racing car which, with Auto-Union, gave Germany Grand Prix dominance in the years immediately prior to the Second World War. Inset: Rudi Caracciola, one of the stars of the German Mercedes team, noted for his brilliant driving in wet conditions. He is seen at the 1938 French Grand Prix at Reims.

'Il Maestro' Nuvolari, Farina, Brivio and Count Trossi; from France, Jean-Pierre Wimille and Raymond Sommer; from South Africa via England, Pat Fairfield. But the favourite to win was the home-based Mauri Rose, and few gave the Europeans a chance against a man good enough to win at Indianapolis.

It did not work out that way. From the flag, Nuvolari in his Alfa shot into the lead and was never headed. He covered the 482.7 km (300 miles) at an average speed of 106.2 kph (66 mph) and finished a comfortable twelve minutes in front of Wimille's Bugatti. Brivio (Alfa), who had suffered from ignition trouble, was third and Sommer, in another Alfa, fourth. Pat Fairfield's ERA was fifth, a remarkable performance in a car outgunned by most of the others on view. Trossi was sixth in a Maserati.

The Vanderbilt Cup revival did not last long. It was run again the following year when the German Bernd Rosemeyer (Auto-Union) won from Dick Seaman (Mercedes) with the American Rex Mays in an Alfa-Romeo third. That proved to be the end of what had started out as a millionaire's dream. Yet in the names of the cars taking part in those two Cup races is encompassed the whole story of Grand Prix racing in the twenties and thirties when Bugatti, Alfa-Romeo,

Mercedes and Auto-Union strode like colossi through the pages of motoring history.

In the USA the concentration was on dirt-track and oval circuit racing, with the famed Indianapolis 500 as the highlight of the year. Great Britain, too, was more or less on the outside, looking in at Grand Prix racing. Apart from a brief flurry by the Sunbeam team at the start of the period, when Segrave won the 1923 and 1924 French and Spanish GPs, British cars were rarely in the picture. In the thirties the ERAs made a hit in light car racing but this, of course, was hardly the same thing as Grand Prix. Instead, most motor-racing interest in Britain centred around Brooklands where hundreds of events were held between the wars, ranging from short sprints to 500 and 1,000 mile events.

On the Continent, the idea of the French Grand Prix was adopted by many other countries and between 1924 and 1934, Grand Prix races were staged in France, Belgium, Switzerland, Germany, Italy, Spain and Monte Carlo. Throughout this period the French Bugattis and Delages and the Italian Alfa-Romeos and Maseratis were very much to the fore. The Bugatti, it is often claimed, was the most successful racing car ever and victory after victory was scored by the products of the Molsheim factory. In fact, from 1928 to 1932, Grand Prix racing was at comparatively low ebb, partly due to the dominance of Bugatti and one or two other makes.

The last five years of peace before the Second World War were vintage ones in the annals of Grand Prix racing. In 1934 the French and Italians were still in command: the French Grand Prix was won by the Monagesque Louis Chiron (later to become the key man in both the Monaco Grand Prix and the famous Monte Carlo Rally) in an Italian Alfa with his team-mates, the Italian Achille Varzi and the Frenchman Guy Moll, second and third. Robert Benoist, another Frenchman, was fourth in a Bugatti.

Inset: The outstanding Italian racing car of the twenties and thirties was the Alfa-Romeo. Sleek in Italian racing red, the model shown is the 1932 P3 version. The larger picture shows the 1935 Derby Maserati, as raced in the United States.

At Spa, in Belgium, Rene Dreyfus (Bugatti) took the honours for France with Brivio (Alfa-Romeo) second and France's Raymond Sommer (Maserati) third. Benoist was again fourth in one of those pale-blue cars distinguished by their horseshoe radiator which reflected another interest of their designer, Ettore Bugatti.

Tripoli was an Alfa benefit, cars driven by Varzi, Moll and Chiron filling the first three places and at Monaco, Moll and Chiron were first and second with Dreyfus bringing a Bugatti in third.

Never again during the pre-war years would the French and Italians bask in such triumphs. Already, in 1934, the writing was on the wall. At the Nurburgring, the German GP was won by Hans Stuck in the strange-looking Auto-Union. The Italian Luigi Fagioli was second in a Mercedes and Italy had to be content with a third place for Alfa and a fourth for Maserati.

The Swiss GP was a similar story, with Auto-Unions first and second and the persistent Dreyfus giving Bugatti a consolation third place. Worst of all for the Italians, their own race fell to the Germans, Mercedes first and Auto-Union second.

It was a portent of 1935. . . .

Led by the great Rudi Caracciola, the Mercedes team swept all before it. The French, Belgian, Swiss and Tripoli races fell to Rudi, and Fagioli took Monaco for Mercedes. With Hans Stuck's victory for Auto-Union in Italy, it should have been a very happy year for the Germans. It would have been, but for an Italian. Nuvolari took his Alfa to the Nurburgring and, unimpressed by Von Brauschitsch setting the fastest lap time in his Mercedes, was vainly chased to the finishing line by Stuck and Rosemeyer in their Auto-Unions and 'Caratsch' in his Mercedes.

It was all too much for the French and Belgians who both ran races for sports cars in 1936 instead of proper Grands Prix (the French also repeated the sports car race in 1937). It did not worry the efficient Germans overmuch. This time Rosemeyer and Stuck made sure of their own Grand Prix and the white cars of the Fatherland cleaned up the remaining major races at Tripoli, Monte Carlo, Bremgarten and Monza.

The following year there could be no pretence that there was any serious opposition to the Germans. It was just a question of which Auto-Union or Mercedes driver would be first to the chequered flag. In Belgium it was Hasse (Auto-Union); at the Nurburgring Caracciola (Mercedes) and in Tripoli, his team-mate

Below: A 1920s 3-litre Bentley. Inset left: A Shell poster. Inset right: Kenneth Evans driving a 1939 Alfa P3 at Brooklands. Right: One of the few cars to uphold British racing prestige in the thirties, the ERA. This is a 1936 version of the Raymond Mays-Humphrey Cook-inspired car.

Lang. Von Brauschitsch won for Mercedes at Monte Carlo but it was the turn of Caracciola in Switzerland and again at Monza.

The pattern continued in 1938, the white cars sweeping all before them. There was no race at Monaco and the Belgians once again reverted to sports cars. The French Grand Prix was revived at Rheims, but the best the French got out of it was a fourth place with Carriere in a 4½-litre Darracq 10 laps behind the Mercedes which were 1-2-3.

In their own Grand Prix the Mercedes were first and second, Auto-Union third and fourth, but there was a slip-up – the winning car was driven by Richard Seaman, the first Englishman to win a major Grand Prix since Segrave in 1923 and 1924, unless one counts the mysterious Anglo-French Bugatti pilot, William Grover, alias 'Williams'.

The war clouds were already gathering when the 1939 motor racing season opened. Again neither the Monaco nor the Italian races were held. At Rheims a Mercedes driven by Lang set the fastest lap and Auto-Unions, in the hands of Muller and Meier, finished first and second. Two 4½-litre Darracqs retrieved a little French honour by coming in third and fourth, albeit three laps behind the winner.

At Spa, in heavy rain, Seaman was leading when he crashed and was killed, but his team-mates, Lang and Von Brauschitsch were first and third, split by the Auto-Union of Hasse. The French driver Raymond Sommer was fourth in an Italian Alfa, three laps behind.

In the German GP 'Caratsch' won for Mercedes with Muller (Auto-Union) second. Pietsch was a lap behind in an outgunned 1½-litre Maserati and Dreyfus in a V12 4½-litre Delahaye another lap behind him.

The Tripoli race was restricted to 1½-litre cars but it made no difference, Lang and Caracciola finishing first and second in V8 Mercedes. Italian honour was partially saved by Villoresi who brought his Alfa in third.

By the following year, Germany was at war and the Italians were able to clean up the Tripoli GP with Alfa Romeos first, second and third.

What was the secret of the German domination of motor racing during the thirties? Firstly, the massive state-aid which meant that Mercedes and Auto-Union were never short of funds or resources. Secondly, Alfred Neubauer, who was probably the greatest team manager of all time and gathered around him some of the greatest drivers of the time. But having said that, the success of Mercedes and Auto-Union has to be put down to sheer mechanical genius. Motor racing organizers were afraid that cars were becoming too fast and too dangerous. They also thought that it was time designers paid more attention to chassis, suspensions and brakes. So for 1934-6 (later extended to 1937) a new formula was devised. It was laid down that all races should be 500 kilometres (312 miles), that engines could be of any size, but that the complete car with empty tanks should weigh not more than 750 kilogrammes (14½ cwt). The authorities thought that engines would remain of moderate size, around 3-litres, and maximum speeds would be restricted to about 241.35 kph (150 mph).

They were wrong. Engines grew to 5 and 6 litres, developing some 600-hp. Light metals and new methods of construction kept the overall weight within the limit, but speeds soared up towards 321 kph (200 mph). Thus the knowledge and skill of the designers, especially the Germans, defeated the rule makers.

In 1938, therefore, a new formula was introduced. Again the objective was to restrain speeds, but this time also to give other constructors a chance against the all-conquering Germans. Engine size was limited to 3-litres supercharged and 4½-litres unsupercharged, the French Darracqs and Delahayes being challengers in this class. A sliding scale of minimum weights was introduced which, it was hoped, would give a chance to 1½-litre cars such as those being successfully produced in England like the ERAs.

But it made no difference to the Germans. They produced 3-litre supercharged versions which, as we have seen, mopped up the opposition just as their bigger brethren had in the previous four years.

Maximum speeds were perhaps lower than with the bigger engined cars, but lap speeds increased since the cars were easier to handle and possessed better brakes so that full use could be made of the acceleration of the engines.

Grand Prix racing represented the cream between the wars, but Indianapolis and Brooklands drew their regular crowds to this specialized form of circuit racing and sports car racing was also a major attraction all over Europe. Italy boasted the famed Mille Miglia, a reminder of the great town-to-town road races, and the Targa Florio. Great Britain had the Tourist Trophy, held through the streets of Newtownards, which is today the oldest surviving motor race although it is now held in England on the Silverstone circuit.

But the greatest and most famous sports car race of them all, another which still survives today, was the Le Mans 24-hour 'Grand Prix de l'endurance'.

For the British, unable to compete on equal terms on the Grand Prix scene, Le Mans was always a major attraction and it probably reached a peak for them in 1929 when, majestically and triumphantly, the Bentleys roared down the finishing straight – 1-2-3-4 – in perfect formation, all wearing British racing green, all on their way to the most resounding victory in the history of this classic event.

It was the culmination of a campaign waged over many races and many years by those who were often

Top: Bugatti, among the most successful French racing cars of all time, with more victories between the wars than any other car. Above: Ferrari and Maserati neck-and-neck, a poster issued by the Automobile Club von Deutschland.

the lone upholders of British racing prestige between the wars, 'The Bentley Boys', as they became known in the popular press.

Their Le Mans odyssey began, in effect, in 1923 when, although Lagache and Leonard were the winners in a Chenard-Walcker, Clement's Bentley set the fastest lap time with a speed in excess of 106.2 kph (66 mph). The following year, with Duff as co-driver, Clement won a neck-and-neck struggle with the Lorraine team and the 1923 winner, Lagache. Only 14 of the 41 starters finished.

In 1925 Clement and Duff were there again in a Bentley, with another car of the same make, driven by Dr Benjafield and Kensington-Moir. The British were now providing a massive challenge to the French cars on their own soil, since they were also represented by Segrave and Duller, Chassagne and 'Sammy' Davis in Sunbeams, and Samuelson and England in an Austin. The Bentleys and Sunbeams set such a pace that most of them cracked up, leaving only the Chassagne-Davis car to limp in second behind a French Lorraine.

It was a similar story the following year. Two of the Bentleys retired (Sunbeam did not enter) and Davis crashed thirty minutes from the finish, leaving the Lorraines to a wonderful 1-2-3 victory.

So to 1927 and a Le Mans always remembered for what happened at the White House corner. . . .

As darkness fell, a French car, driven by Tabourin, crashed just beyond the White House and partially blocked the road. Callingham (Bentley) came full speed round the corner to find his way barred. In a desperate effort to avoid the Frenchman, he went into the ditch, rolled over and effectively closed most of what little space remained. Right behind him was his team-mate, George Duller, flat out as usual, and straight into the wreckage he went.

When Davis cornered in the third Bentley it seemed that the whole team would be eliminated but, as he saw the chaos in front of him, he slammed on his brakes, slid broadside into the other cars, backed away and crawled on with his damaged car.

Behind him, the disasters continued as two more cars smashed into the wreckage. In the pits all was consternation and confusion as teams waited for cars which did not come. Then into view limped the Davis Bentley and pulled into the pits. A quick examination and it was decided that it was safe for the car to continue, although all hope of victory had disappeared. Jean Chassagne, driving this time for Aries, had taken full advantage of the pile-up to gain a commanding lead.

Away slithered the damaged Bentley, yet magically every time round it picked up speed and when Benjafield took over the wheel after 344.33 km (214 miles) it was travelling healthily. The Aries was still far out in front but now W.O. Bentley, the team chief and designer of what Bugatti is alleged to have called 'the fastest lorries in the world', took a desperate gamble and ordered Benjafield to go flat out. It came off. Under pressure, it was the blue Aries which cracked and the surviving Bentley, against all the odds, went on to win.

In 1928, the French were forced to take a back seat in their own race which developed into a straight fight between the USA, making a rare foray into Europe, and Great Britain. Chrysler and Stutz represented the USA and pitted against them were the pick of British sports-racers, Alvis, Aston-Martin, Lagonda and, of course, Bentley.

In this race, another incident occurred which has been remembered through the years. For the first, and last, time the Bentleys did not carry jacks and the inevitable happened. The car shared by Birkin and Chassagne had a puncture miles from the pits. Birkin hacked the useless rubber away and drove on the rim until that too collapsed. Then he ran to the pits whereupon the gallant Chassagne, fast approaching his fiftieth birthday, shouldered a jack and spare and

Above: A famous German car, the 1938 BMW 327. The marque is highly regarded today. Left: Von Brauschistch driving a Mercedes during the Swiss Grand Prix. Below: Hermann Lang (Mercedes) at Reims in 1939. Lang survived the war to make a demonstration run at the re-opening of Donington Circuit. Bottom: Another shot of the 1938 Swiss Grand Prix.

ran all the way back to the car to get her mobile again. The effort was rewarded. Entering the last lap, Birkin needed to break the circuit record to qualify the car for the following year – and he did just that.

Meanwhile the Bentley, which had been the first of the team to crash the year before and was now being driven by the team's millionaire backer, Babe Barnato and Rubin, went on to win. The Americans filled the next three places with another Bentley fifth and an Alvis sixth, so honours were pretty much divided between the States and Britain.

Bentley went all out for a hat-trick in 1929 and two teams totalling five cars were entered. One team comprised Barnato and 'Tim' Birkin, Jack Dunfee and Glen Kidston and Clement and Chassagne. The other had Earl Howe and Rubin and Count d'Erlanger and Benjafield.

Howe's car was forced to retire but the others were never headed and filled the first four places, Barnato and Birkin in the winning car, covering 2,843 kilometres (1,767 miles) at an average 118.47 kph (73.63 mph).

There was to be one more victorious year for 'The Bentley Boys'. In 1930, two teams were again entered, the official works team and another, led by Birkin and sponsored by millionairess racehorse owner, Miss Dorothy Paget. Barnato and Kidston came first with Watney and Clement second. It was a good note on which to end the story. Lack of finance killed official Bentley participation after that and Dorothy Paget also withdrew her support.

The withdrawal of Bentley gave other marques a look-in and in 1931, Alfa-Romeo gained victory for Italy. Ironically, the car was driven by Earl Howe and Sir Henry Birkin. It was an all-Italian victory the following year, with Chinetti driving an Alfa. Chinetti repeated his success in 1934 with the Frenchman Philippe Etancelin as his co-driver but the British were back with a vengeance, Rileys being second and third and an MG Magnette fourth. Sixteen of the 23 cars which finished were British.

It was a good omen for 1935 when once again a green car was first across the line, this time a Lagonda with Luis Fontes and J.S. Hindmarsh sharing the wheel. Le Mans was to be the scene of many more international struggles, but there was, of course, a ten year gap, 1939 to 1949, caused by the Second World War.

What were the great racing cars of the inter-war period? Most makes have their devotees but few could quarrel with:

2-litre, 6-cylinder Fiat (Type 804) which won the French Grand Prix of 1922. . . .

1923 Mercedes 2-litre Indianapolis model, whose claim to fame is being the first Formula-sized supercharged racing car. . . .

1923 Sunbeam, which owed much to the 1922 Fiat, being a 2-litre, 6-cylinder, unsupercharged car which finished first, second and fourth in the French Grand Prix. . . .

1923 Miller, a multi-carburettor, unsupercharged

2-litre straight-eight, winner of the Indianapolis 500 which Miller designs were to influence for many years. . . .

1924 P2 Alfa-Romeo, a 2-litre supercharged straight-eight which won the Grands Prix of Europe in 1924 and 1925, the Italian Grands Prix in 1924 and 1925 and the Targa Florio in 1930. . . .

Bugatti Type 35, 1924 to 1930, the single ohc, straight-eight, both unsupercharged and supercharged 2- and 2.3-litres, one of the most successful road racing cars of all time with victories too numerous to list. . . .

1925 Delage, with a V12, 2-litre supercharged engine, winner of the French and Spanish GPs of 1925. . . .

1927 Delage, supercharged straight-eight which dominated the 1926–7 $1\frac{1}{2}$-litre Grand Prix formula. . . .

1930 Maserati, 8-cylinder, $2\frac{1}{2}$-litre supercharged car which was the fastest thing on the circuits that year. . . .

1931 Bugatti Type 51, a 2.3-litre, twin ohc, won the French, Monaco and Belgian GPs in 1931 and continued a winner until 1933. . . .

1932 Alfa-Romeo, the famous Type B monoposto, which won over 40 races between 1932 and 1935. . . .

1934–5 Type W25 Mercedes-Benz which won 12 major races in 2 seasons. . . .

1935 ERA, the British 6-cylinder $1\frac{1}{2}$-litre which gained many international successes in the voiturette class between 1935 and 1938 and after the war put up some valiant struggles in Grand Prix races. . . .

1936–7 Auto-Union, a highly unconventional car in which the 16-cylinder, more than 6-litre engine, was mounted behind the driver; it won many races but was always a difficult car to handle. . . .

1937 Mercedes-Benz, the most powerful Grand Prix car ever built, won the Tripoli, German, Monaco, Swiss, Italian and Czech Grands Prix in 1937, its 3-litre successor won 6 Grands Prix in 1939.

Below: A 1939 Maserati 4CL.

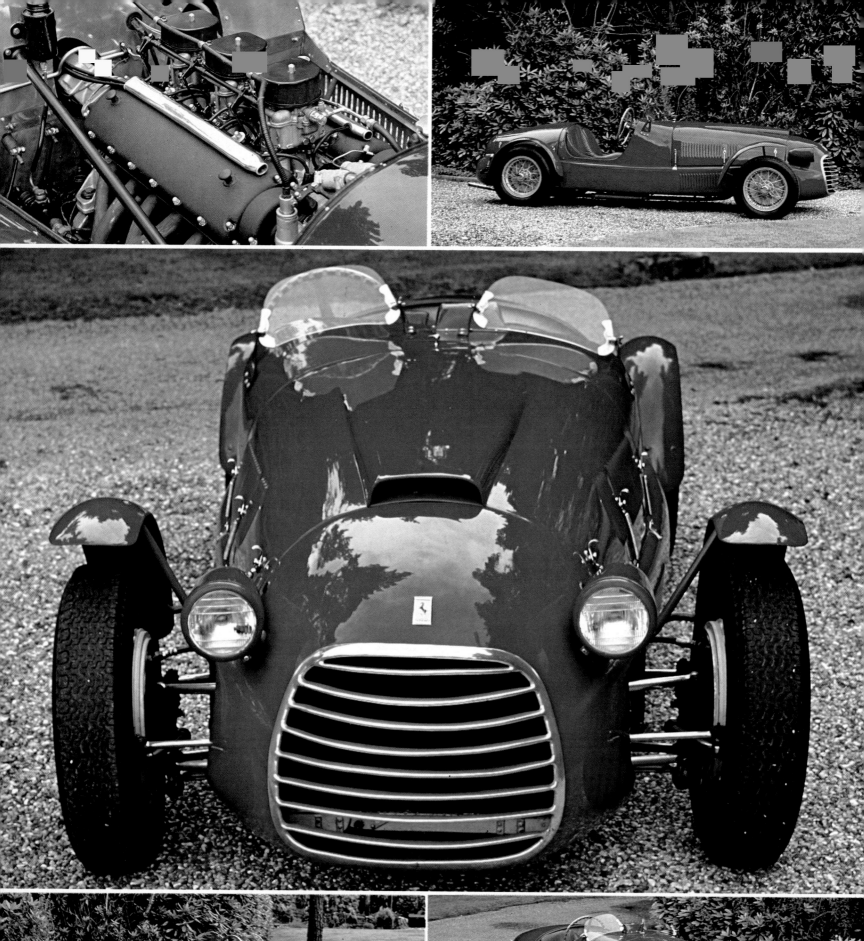

Motor Racing– The International Years

Motor racing became truly international in the late fall of 1978. In that year, an Italian–American named Mario Andretti became World Grand Prix Champion, the second United States citizen (Phil Hill in 1961 was the first) to achieve the distinction. Neither drove an American car. Andretti was at the wheel of a British Lotus; Hill a works driver for the Italian Ferrari organization. There was, however, more to the internationalization than the achievements of one man, or one team.

The years following the Second World War proved topsy-turvey ones for motoring and motor sport. The aftermath of war left very few manufacturers in a good position to produce new cars and even fewer who could spare the time to develop race cars. Eventually matters sorted themselves out and motor sport became a major attraction in most parts of the world 'from Singapore to Moscow via Dayton, Ohio'.

Although things gradually settled down, only one man remained a constant factor in modern motor sport, an Italian named Enzo Ferrari. A former Alfa-Romeo team driver and team manager, Il Commend-atore presented the first Formula One Ferrari to the world in 1948. Thirty years later, Ferrari had 71 World Championship Grand Prix victories and eight World Championships.

When his cars made their début at Valentino Park in 1948 they were 12-cylinder 1,500-cc machines driven by a Frenchman, Raymond Sommer, an Italian, 'Nino' Farina, and a Siamese, 'B. Bira'. Sommer finished third, the other two retired. Not a great beginning. But. . . .

In 1949, the cars from Maranello dominated the Grand Prix scene in the absence of Alfa-Romeo, but unfortunately for Ferrari and his star driver, Alberto Ascari, the World Championship had not yet been instituted.

The 1948 Ferrari 166. Enzo Ferrari, who drove for and managed Alfa-Romeo in the thirties, emerged as the dominant figure of Italian motor racing after the Second World War and his cars, almost alone, upheld Italian Grand Prix prestige.

Ferrari's first World Championship victory came in 1951 when, in the British Grand Prix at Silverstone, a brilliant solo effort by the Argentinian, Froilan Gonzales, vanquished the Alfas. His car, the 375, a $4\frac{1}{2}$-litre V12, was to become one of the legendary cars in motor racing history. Spectacular driver though he was, Gonzales scored only one other GP win and that too was in the British event in 1954 and again in a Ferrari.

Throughout 1952 and 1953, largely due to the insistence of the French, the Grands Prix were held for Formula 2 cars. It made little difference to Ferrari. His driver, Ascari, and his car, the 2-litre, 4-cylinder 500, were in a class of their own. The famous son of a famous father dominated the 1952 series and won every Grand Prix except the Swiss – in which he did not take part.

It was much the same story in 1953, except that one race kindled the imagination of many who had never attended a motor race and gave the sport a much-needed shot in the arm. The event was the French Grand Prix, that year at the Rheims circuit, a high-speed triangle cut through the flat, unwooded country-side of northern France. It looked like an Italian holiday. The all-conquering four-cylinder Ferraris were accompanied by five brand-new Maseratis. It was rumoured that the just-modified engines of the latter would give them a slightly higher speed than the Ferraris, especially on the straights, an important factor on the Rheims circuit.

Against these nine powerful Italian machines most of the others could only hope. Jean Behra, French champion and former motor-cycle king, who had beaten the Italians in 1952, was there, backed by Manzon and Simon. And France also had the veteran former champion, Louis Rosier.

The chances for France seemed brighter than those of Britain whose idol, Stirling Moss, was driving a Cooper-Alta; or Belgium, whose champion, the trumpet-playing bandleader, Johnny Claes, was at the wheel of a British Connaught. Baron de Graffenreid, the Swiss champion was also taking part, driving his own Maserati.

The Italians, however, seemed to have it all their own way, with the best cars and, Stirling Moss apart, also the best drivers. Maserati pinned their faith on two Argentinian drivers, Gonzalez and former world champion, Juan Manuel Fangio, 'El Chueco', or 'Old Bandy Legs'. Ferrari, on the other hand, had the reigning world champion, Ascari and two other great Italian drivers, Farina and Villoresi. Completing the four-car team was a young and relatively inexperienced English driver, Mike Hawthorn.

From the start Gonzalez took the lead in a breathtaking demonstration of sheer speed. Behind him a string of Ferraris gave vain chase. And so it went on, lap after lap. At the halfway mark the Argentinian stopped for fuel and the Ferrari team realized they had been duped – the Maserati had started the race with a half-empty fuel tank, giving the car a precious weight advantage which had enabled Gonzalez to build up a lead. More importantly, he had forced the Ferraris to drive beyond their limits, a potentially disastrous course. However, Hawthorn, Villoresi and Ascari, at 1-2-3, looked comfortably in command. But behind them, the Maserati pit signalled to Fangio, in effect, 'Gonzalez has done his stuff – now it's up to you'.

'El Chueco' needed little urging. Steaming through the field he passed Ascari, then Villoresi, and when Hawthorn looked around it was the Argentinian and not his team-mates on his tail. Nor was Gonzalez out of the reckoning. Flat out, he regained most of the places lost by his stop and was soon breathing down the necks of Hawthorn and Fangio.

The two leaders stormed around, seemingly locked together, with Gonzalez charging along behind. Wild with excitement the crowd watched the three cars go into the last lap, and then the last corner, with Fangio only a few feet ahead. But the Maserati wavered a little, Hawthorn rammed his foot down – and crossed the line, winner by one second. Fangio beat his team-mate, Gonzalez, by only half that margin – one of the closest motor races of all time. Hawthorn, youngest driver ever to win a Grand Prix, joined the then small band of British major Grand Prix winners: Segrave, 'Williams' and Seaman.

For Ferrari, the next few years were to have more downs than ups. German industry had made a rapid recovery from the war and once again the powerful Mercedes were seen on the Grand Prix circuits. The Germans had always sought the finest drivers, whatever their nationality, and now they had the best pair in the world, Fangio and the young British driver, Stirling Moss. 1955 was a Mercedes benefit year and only at Monaco, where the French driver, Maurice Trintignant, held off Castellotti in a Lancia, did Ferrari chalk up a win.

Mercedes successes were not confined to GP events. Moss, with journalist Denis Jenkinson alongside him, won the great Mille Miglia road race.

In 1956 Lancia withdrew from racing after Ascari

lost his life, and Fangio wound up driving a Lancia-Ferrari, Il Commendatore having acquired the $2\frac{1}{2}$-litre V8 cars from the Turin company. Fangio's British Grand Prix win in one of these machines was not to be repeated the following year, as Ferrari failed to win a single race. In 1958 Hawthorn won the World Championship for them, but his team-mates, English Peter Collins, and Italian Luigi Musso, both lost their lives. The tragic story continued when Hawthorn, after retiring from racing, crashed and was killed in his Jaguar on the Guildford by-pass.

Another Englishman, Tony Brooks, who had first made a name by winning the Syracuse Grand Prix for the British Connaught firm, became Ferrari team-leader in 1959, winning the French and German races. In 1960 Maranello ran updated 246 Dino cars for Phil Hill, an American, Wolfgang von Trips, from Germany, and Belgium's Willy Mairesse. Hill scored the team's only victory, appropriately enough in the Italian Grand Prix. The season ended an era because, in 1961, Ferrari joined the British-led switch to rear-engined cars, sweeping all before them. In the British Grand Prix at Aintree 'Taffy' von Trips led the team to a 1-2-3 victory and he also won the Dutch event. But, with the World Championship in his grasp, he

Left: One of the early post-War attempts to produce an outstanding British racing car – the Cooper-Alta. Below: Maserati had their moments of glory in the thirties and again after the War. In action here is the 4387cc 1948 model.

was killed in the Italian GP. Phil Hill went on to win the race for Ferrari and the world title for himself, the first American to do so.

A new Ferrari appeared in 1963. It was the 'Aero' design, and proved remarkably fast although not always reliable. The following year, the former World Motor Cycling Champion, John Surtees, driving the $1\frac{1}{2}$-litre V8 Ferrari Type 158, won the German and Italian Grands Prix and took the world championship.

The years went by with the blood-red Ferraris upholding the prestige of Italy. Drivers came and went. Bandini, probably the best Italian driver of his period, was fatally burned at Monaco in 1967. For three seasons, the New Zealander, Chris Amon, was the team-leader. It was in 1968, during his period as team-leader, that Ferrari cars first appeared with wings and aerofoils.

New and Old Worlds met in 1971 and 1972 when Italian-born American champion Mario Andretti drove occasionally for Ferrari. Driving the 312B model, he scored his first Grand Prix win in South Africa in 1971. The previous year, the Belgian Jackie Ickx had been close to winning the world title with Ferrari but he never came so close again, the 312B2 which followed the highly successful 312B never being as competitive as its predecessor.

Great years were to return for Il Commendatore. An Austrian driver, Niki Lauda, who had had little success driving with March and other cars, joined the team in 1974 and on his début, driving the 312B3,

Previous pages: Night at Le Mans, 1953: Roy Nockold's painting of the winning Jaguar of Tony Rolt and Duncan Hamilton. Above: 1955 Maserati 250F. Left: Moss (Maserati) at Monaco, 1956. Below: Hawthorn (Ferrari) at the German Grand Prix of 1957. Right: Fangio (Ferrari) in the 1956 Syracuse Grand Prix. Inset top: Andretti (Ferrari) in the 1972 Spanish Grand Prix at Jarama. Inset bottom: Siffert (BRM) leads Regazzoni (Ferrari) in the 1971 German Grand Prix.

finished second. He went on to win 14 Grands Prix for Ferrari before leaving them at the end of 1977. The 1975 312T was the car which contributed most to his success. He completely dominated that season and won the first of his two world titles by a big margin.

The Argentinian, Carlos Reutemann, joined Ferrari in 1976, taking over as team-leader when Lauda went. He contributed five GP victories before leaving for Lotus at the end of the 1978 season.

But if the white-haired genius of Maranello has been the one constant factor in Grand Prix motor-racing since 1949, it is the rags to riches story of British racing car manufacturers – and their engine suppliers – which has been the dominant factor in the sport.

During the early years after the War Alfa-Romeo, and to a lesser extent Maserati, were supreme. The French and the Germans slowly came back into the picture, but the British were still struggling with a few brave efforts like the HWM team, to which Stirling Moss graduated after serving his apprenticeship in 500 cc racing, and the Connaught team, which was in due course to achieve some measure of success in Grand Prix racing. HWM used Alta power units; Connaught, originally a Lea-Francis based engine.

Unable to compete in the Grand Prix field, the hard-up British had thrown their enthusiasm into a new form of motor-racing, small cars mostly powered by motor-cycle engines. 'Half-litre', or 500 cc, racing rapidly became popular, not only in Great Britain but

also on the Continent and as far afield as Singapore.

Soon the most successful manufacturers of these machines were a father and son partnership, Charles and John Cooper. They moved into the world of Grand Prix racing and soon the rear-engined Coopers were championship contenders, powered with what was to become one of the most outstanding racing engines, the Coventry-Climax, made by a firm better-known for making fire-engines. Cooper also discovered two great drivers, an Australian, 'Black Jack' Brabham, who was to win one world title after another, and a New Zealander, Bruce MacLaren. Both were later to manufacture top racing cars under their own names, although MacLaren was tragically killed whilst testing a car at Goodwood.

Around the time the Coopers were emerging, a leading industrialist, Tony Vandervell, saddened at the abortive attempts of BRM to establish a British national team, bought a Ferrari, christened it *The Thinwall Special*, and went on to develop his own Vanwall cars which were to win the World Manufacturers Championship.

For the first time since Grand Prix racing began early in the century, British cars and drivers bestrode the scene. In the wake of the Cooper, the Vanwall and the Connaught, came Lotus, a now viable BRM, Tyrrell, March, MacLaren and Brabham, together with a string of great British and Commonwealth drivers – Brabham, MacLaren, two more New Zealanders, Denny Hulme and Chris Amon, Jim Clark, Jackie Stewart, John Surtees, Mike Hawthorn, Stuart Lewis-Evans, Stirling Moss, Graham Hill, Tony Brooks, James Hunt. . . .

The Climax engines were now being used by many manufacturers and when the Coventry firm decided to

Above: The British Grand Prix at Brands Hatch in 1978. Inset: The driving position of a 1966 Formula One Lotus. Right: The Monaco Grand Prix: Jim Clark corners in his Lotus.

pull out of motor racing, Grand Prix teams in general, and British ones in particular, were in a grave dilemma.

Colin Chapman, of Lotus, found the man, engine designer Keith Duckworth, and the finance, from the Ford Motor Company. The resulting Cosworth engine (from the names of the partners in the firm making it: Mike Costin and Keith Duckworth) became even more successful than the Climax and, as the 1978 season drew to its close, had no less than 118 Grand Prix wins to its credit. Moreover, variations of the Cosworth were being used to a great extent in the United States and Canada, and when the American USAC racers came to Europe in 1978, most of them had Cosworth power-units under the hood.

In fact, when Al Unser, in 1978, won his third Indianapolis 500 he was driving a British Lola car, powered by a British Cosworth engine.

At last, international motor racing was truly international.

Cars of Today and Tomorrow

As the 1980s dawned, car manufacturers were all, in their own ways, seeking the answer to the question: what will the car of the future be like?

The trends were towards turbo-charging, four-wheel drive, anti-lock braking, air dams and hatchback styling. The Swedish SAAB was well advanced with turbo-charging and so was the British specialist builder, Panther. The Russians introduced a chunky little car, the Lada Niva, which showed that they were no longer slow to learn, as it had both four-wheel drive and hatchback styling. Vauxhall filled gaps in their range by moving into higher quality cars with the Carlton and the Royale, but the really interesting feature of these General Motors products was the use of air dams.

There were cars designed for ease and comfort – the Lancia Beta with automatic transmission, for instance; and others seeking performance, like the Japanese Colt with eight-speed gearbox. Some sought both, like the open two-seater from Italy's Pininfarina based upon the Jaguar XJS. In the USA, the sporty

Left: Rear view of 1973 Renault 5TL. Below: The Ford Fiesta which made a successful sporting debut in the famed Monte Carlo event of 1979.

line was being pushed by Chevrolet with the Camaro Z28, the Camaro Berlinetta, the Monza Spyder and the Corvette which, after 26 years in production, was still being advertised as America's only true production sports car. The racing brothers Chevrolet who pioneered the marque would have been proud. But Buick, also under the GM banner, were content, like Rolls-Royce in England, to emphasize that motoring was for enjoyment. The 1979 Buick Regal, for instance, was advertised as 'The difference between a car you like and a car you love'.

Suppliers of materials, parts and accessories have been no less eager to explore the future. The Bayer K67, constructed in 1967, was an experimental car designed to demonstrate new engineering materials to the car industry. In less time than it takes to tell, features of the Bayer were being incorporated in production models, amongst them the Triumph TR7, the Ford RS 2000, the Rover 3500 (Car of the Year 1977) and the Porsche 928 (Car of the Year 1978).

In 1978, Triplex, the safety glass firm, unveiled their version of the car of tomorrow: The 10–20 Glassback. A stylish estate car, based upon the Austin Morris Princess, the appearance was drastically changed by the Ogle design unit with an all-glass estate area at the rear. Designed to stimulate interest in glass as a medium for increased motoring safety, convenience and visual appeal, the Glassback has a vandal-resistant windscreen, 'invisible' radio aerial and de-icing and demisting system and a glass sun roof, very thin (2.3 mm) and yet so strong that it can be opened for ventilation by flexing the glass. The door glasses – 3 mm – are as thin as can be made without flutter.

To make the aerial, demister and de-icer invisible one of the inner glass surfaces of the superlaminated windscreen has a transparent metal-oxide coating which doubles as a radio aerial and windscreen demister/de-icer. Originally developed for aircraft like the Boeing 747 and Concorde, the windscreen can be converted to the desired purpose at a flick of a switch.

Another aspect of tomorrow's car to receive atten-

Above: A modern American luxury car, the 1976 Cadillac Seville. Inset: The aptly-named Stingray, otherwise known as the 1963 Chevrolet Corvette. Right: The 1975 Porsche Turbo, with a glimpse of the turbocharger itself.

tion is cost. The Ford Company won a Design Council Award with their Fiesta because of its low maintenance requirements. The Fiesta features items like a self-adjusting clutch, a single-piece exhaust system secured by only two bolts, and natural break lines between the body panels to allow for part repairing and respraying instead of having to respray the whole car. But modern car designers should be humbled to remember the modest Jowett, manufactured in Bradford, England, some 50 years ago, which had hinged floor boards for access to the transmission, a screw-cap dip-stick which avoided the need for oily, mucky rags when checking the oil, and many other features ahead of its time.

Yet over these developments hung a dark shadow: the world energy crisis. All over the globe, men were drilling for oil – in the sandy deserts of Saudi Arabia, below the cruel grey waves of the North Sea, in the rolling acres of Texas and beneath the sun-kissed breakers off Florida, even in the picture postcard countryside of Dorset, England.

However much they found, there was always the question: how long will it last? The answers varied from the optimistic 'Indefinitely' to the pessimistic, like British politician Roy Jenkins, who saw no future whatsoever for the traditional motor car relying upon petrol and oil.

Nearly everyone agreed, however, that the time must come when the world would have to take a very serious look at the energy crisis. In the short term, increased efficiency of the internal combustion engine could provide a partial and limited answer: fuel injection so that less fuel was wasted; turbo charging to get more performance from the same amount of fuel; and re-designed engines. This last applied especially to the Wankel, or rotary engines, which were just beginning to make an impact on world markets when the fuel crisis first reared its ugly head. Despite the many advantages of the rotary engine, fuel economy was not one of them. Japanese engineers, in particular the Mazda firm which had led the way in installing rotary engines in their cars, redesigned and improved the engine so as to meet the new and demanding standards of fuel economy.

In the long term, any motor car using petrol and oil would pose a threat to the world's energy resources. So what could replace the internal combustion engine?

Most engineers agreed that steam was out. Although the steam carriage and locomotive had been the predecessor of the car and although steam cars had once held the world land speed record, the requirements in terms of water and boiler size, plus the need to get up steam before setting off on each journey, ruled out a return to the steam car.

But what about electricity? Again the world record had once belonged to electric cars and most experts agreed that a return to electricity was feasible – providing the storage battery problem could be overcome.

Relying as they must on batteries, the present range of any electric car is limited and after, say, 50 miles, the batteries must be replaced or re-charged. The disadvantages of this are obvious. In other respects, the advantages of the electric car are great and research and development is now world-wide.

In the United States, in 1969, General Motors presented a report, 'Progress of Power', covering alternative sources of power for vehicles of the future.

Two years later, the Lunar Rover, the first vehicle to be driven on the moon, used a mobility system designed and built by GM's Delco Electronics Division.

International conferences on electric vehicles are now held annually. In Europe, the Electricity Council of the United Kingdom, Electricité de France and Rheinische Westfalisches Elektrizitatswerk of the Federal Republic of Germany, have a co-operative agreement for promoting the development of electrical vehicles.

In Germany, 20 electrically-powered buses in Düsseldorf and Mönchengladbach covered 2.5 million km (1.5 million miles) and carried 25 million passengers. Some 130 electric vans ran nearly 0.8 million km (0.5 million miles).

In England, 62 battery vans were used in a scheme by the Department of Industry and the Greater London Council. They were to be monitored for performance, fuel consumption, running costs and driver reaction to see how they compared with diesel or petrol-driven vehicles. Most had a range of about 50 miles without changing batteries and could operate comfortably at 40 mph. Acceleration was said to be at least comparable with similar conventional vehicles.

Two British cars of distinction: the 1978 Rolls-Royce
Camargue and a 1976 Rover 3500.

The 'plus', of course, was that the vehicles were silent and fume-free, a major environmental advantage in big cities like London.

Those cynical about the prospects for electric cars might heed the results already achieved by Lucas, one of the world's major electronic and components companies. At Brands Hatch in 1976, on the occasion of the British Grand Prix, a Lucas Electric Taxi set an official record lap speed record for electric vehicles, covering the 4.21 km (2.6136 mile) Grand Prix circuit in a time of 3 minutes 16.04 seconds at an average speed of 77.22 kph (47.99 mph). The Taxi has a top speed approaching 96.54 kph (60 mph) and a range of nearly 161 km (100 miles) on a single charge. The cost is a fraction of the cost of petrol or diesel fuel.

The Lucas-modified Seddon midi-bus became the first battery electric vehicle to be driven non-stop between two English cities when, officially observed by the RAC, it journeyed from Birmingham to Manchester, a distance of 148.03 km (92 miles) at an average speed of 48.27 kph (30 mph). Lucas have also built electric vans and personnel carriers.

The Electricity Council has road tested 66 Enfield 8000 electric cars over a 3-year period for a fleet mileage of 200,000. Many minor problems were ironed out, but the battery remained the major item requiring development. Even so, the Council felt that 30 per cent of road traffic could be electric. Other reports have suggested a figure as high as 70 per cent. It is also possible that cars could have power sources, combining both electricity and conventional fuel.

Perhaps the last word on the cars of tomorrow should be left to Henry Ford II.

He says that at one time the *Wall Street Journal* forecast transportation in the year 2000 as a dazzling

Above: Cars in cities – two designs for little runabout cars for use in city centres, easy to park and causing little congestion. **Right:** This eye-catching custom car was originally a 1940's American Dodge.

Buck Rogers-like world of plush, electronically-controlled ground vehicles and 6,000 mph air-liners. Now the *Journal* has modified its view and says that today's airline passenger or motorist should be able to step into a vehicle of the early 21st century and feel right at home.

Of the energy crisis, Ford drily comments: 'Nobody knows how much oil is left in the ground. And the chances are that we will never find out because we will never get to the bottom of the barrel. We know that more oil is discovered every year than is used and more has been discovered in recent years than ever before.'

If Henry Ford II is correct, then the motor car as we know it is likely to be around for a good many years.

The Record Breakers

The World Land Speed Record did not – for many years – exist officially. There were International Class Records for different types of car, covering distances, durations and different types of engine. In practice, the fastest speeds have been attained by the most powerful cars over the shortest distances and so 'world land speed records' were set over the flying kilometre and the flying mile. The comparatively recent intro-duction of jet cars has meant that there are now two world records – one for conventional cars, conven-tional in that they have direct drive to the wheels; and the other for jet cars which rely on the thrust and impetus of their engines and have no direct drive to the wheels.

The first car to hold the record was electric. One of the founder members of the French Automobile Club, the oldest in the world, was the Marquis de Chasseloup-Laubat. He designed an electric car, the *Jeantaud*, and with his brother, the Comte Gaston, at the controls, the car covered a kilometre at the then sensational speed of 63.14 kph (39.24 mph). That was in December 1898.

A few weeks later – in January 1899 – Camille Jenatzy, a red-bearded Belgian who later earned a reputation as a Gordon Bennett and Grand Prix driver, turned up at the same venue, Achères, near Paris, and with an electric car of his own design set a new record at 66.64 kph (41.42 mph).

Gaston promptly did better with 70.30 kph (43.69 mph).

Jenatzy found bigger and better batteries to achieve a speed of 80.32 kph (49.92 mph).

Gaston did likewise and pushed the record up to 92.68 kph (57.60 mph).

At this point the French Automobile Club decided it was time to impose a set of rules and appoint official timekeepers. The Chasseloup brothers bowed out of the scene, leaving the stage to Jenatzy and his car, *La Jamais Contente* (*The Never Content*), allegedly named

after his wife. In this vehicle, shaped like a torpedo, the Belgian set a shattering record of 105.86 kph (65.79 mph).

This was a truly remarkable speed for 1899 when the car, whatever its motive power, was still in its infancy. Not surprisingly, there was a lull until 1902 when a steam car smashed the record. Leon Serpollet, whose cars still run in veteran events, literally steamed along the Promenade des Anglais at Nice at 120.68 kph (75 mph).

It was, however, an American who made an impact on the record scene with a car powered by an internal combustion engine. Millionaire W.K. Vanderbilt, driving a Mercedes-Simplex, equalled Jenatzy's record, but was nearly 16 kph (10 mph) slower than Serpollet. Not to be defeated, Vanderbilt switched to a Mors, one of the type which competed in the 1902 Paris–Vienna race, and in this proven racer he became the new record-holder at 122.41 kph (76.08 mph).

Other drivers jumped on the band-wagon and Henry Fournier, in a specially-modified Mors, pushed the record up to 123.2 kph (76.6 mph). He held the record less than a month before Augieres, also in a Mors, clocked 124.10 kph (77.13 mph).

A giant 100-hp Gobron-Brillie, nicknamed *Gobbling Billie*, was next to take the record. Driven by Arthur Duray on a measured strip at Ostend in July, 1903, *Gobbling Billie* pushed the figures up to 134.30 kph (83.47 mph) and a few months later, at Dourdan, to 136.33 kph (84.73 mph).

Meanwhile, in the USA, Henry Ford recorded a speed of 147.01 kph (91.37 mph) and Vanderbilt one of 148.51 kph (92.30 mph). At the time, the Auto-mobile Club of America was not recognized by the international controlling body, which consequently refused to accept either claim as a world record. It was a very unsatisfactory state of affairs and there must have been some relief, in European hearts at least, when in March 1904, *Gobbling Billie*, this time with Louis Rigolly at the controls, beat official and un-official records twice in one day, first at 149.96 kph (93.20 mph) and then at 152.50 kph (94.78 mph).

Percy Lambert (Talbot) on the Byfleet banking at Brooklands on his way to clock 100 miles in an hour.

Rigolly did not hold the record for long. Baron Pierre de Caters, who had been racing some ten years without a major victory, wheeled his Gordon-Bennett Mercedes out at Ostend and returned 156.49 kph (97.26 mph). His luck had changed for in the same year – 1904 – he was first in the Circuit des Ardennes.

Gobbling Billie was not yet finished. The car which had already twice held the world record took it again in July, 1904. Rigolly was the driver, Ostend the venue and the speed a breathtaking 166.63 kph (103.56 mph).

In November another 100-hp car took over: a Darracq, driven by P. Baras, winner of the 1899 Paris to Ostend race. The Darracq was not much faster than the Gobron-Brillie at 168.18 kph (104.53 mph) and that figure was soon under unofficial fire from the USA, where a young Englishman, Arthur Macdonald, clocked 168.38 kph (104.65 mph) in a Napier, while Herbert Bowden, in a Mercedes-engined car, registered 176.59 kph (109.75 mph). The Americans recognized Macdonald's figure as a world record but not Bowden's, since his car exceeded the weight limit laid down for Grand Prix cars. Although now it is difficult to see what the regulations for Grand Prix racing had to do with world record-breaking. But the argument was academic, since the international authorities again refused to recognize either Macdonald or Bowden. Recognized or not, Bowden's car started a trend since it was the first specially-built car to enter the lists and in later years all world-record aspirants were to be 'specials'. Bowden's machine featured a specially constructed long chassis with two 60-hp Mercedes engines, set in tandem.

Back in Europe, Victor Hemery set a new official record in a monster Darracq of 200-hp. On a stretch of road between Arles and Salon, his speed of 176.43 kph (109.65 mph) was fractionally below Bowden's unofficial figure. Hemery, however, was about to challenge the Americans on their own territory and, in 1906, he took the Darracq across the Atlantic to the Daytona Speed Trials. The beach at Daytona was to play a major part in the world record story and 1906 proved no exception.

Hemery lost his record, but not to Ford, Vanderbilt, Macdonald or Bowden. The new holder was a *steam* car, a Stanley Steamer driven by Frank Marriott. The chassis was the standard 10 hp production model Stanley Steamer, but with a specially-made boiler designed to withstand much higher steam pressures than normal. A streamlined body, rather similar to the Grand Prix cars of the time, was fitted. This car became the first to take the record at more than two miles a minute, Marriott clocking 195.61 kph (121.57 mph) over the kilometre and 205.40 kph (127.66 mph) over the mile. For some reason, the international authorities chose to recognize only the lower speed. Even so, it was to stand for nearly four years, but it was the last time the world record was held by a steam car.

The next record was to be the subject of controversy. It was set by Victor Hemery, driving a Blitzen-Benz, at Brooklands in 1909. Hemery passed Marriott's kilometre record but failed to equal his unrecognized time over the mile. At the half-mile, however, he was timed at 205.770 kph (127.887 mph). It was the first time the record had been set at Brooklands, the first time a petrol-engined car had taken the record at more than two miles a minute and the *last* time a record was permitted on the evidence of a run in one direction only. Afterwards it was decreed that all short-distance records must be established on the mean time of two runs over the course, one in each direction.

Meanwhile, another disputed claim came from the USA, where America's top motor sport personality, Barney Oldfield, travelled at 211.94 kph (131.72 mph) at Daytona.

Another four years passed. Then, on the eve of the First World War, a Briton, L.G. Hornsted, driving a colossal 21,504 cc Benz, became the first record-holder under the new rules. His speed for the two runs was 199.68 kph (124.10 mph), but Hemery's record was demolished anyway since the faster of Hornsted's two runs was 206.21 kph (128.16 mph).

Hornsted's record survived until May 1922, when Kenelm Lee Guinness, whose initials were taken for the name of one of the world's leading sparking-plugs, KLG, drove an 18,322 cc Sunbeam at a speed of 215.20 kph (133.75 mph) at Brooklands. It was the last time the record was set at Brooklands, for the track simply was not fast enough for the more powerful record-breakers gradually being developed.

The next chapter in the story featured an Anglo-French duel between England's Ernest Eldridge and France's René Thomas. Eldridge had a FIAT, powered by a 21-litre aircraft engine, and it must have been a terrifying sight as it sped along the narrow course at Arpajon, France, Eldridge's passenger hanging on for dear life. Eldridge's mean speed was 236.57 kph (147.03 mph), but Thomas could manage only 230.55 kph (143.29 mph). The Frenchman, however, complained that Eldridge's car did not comply with the regulations as it was not fitted with reverse gear. With his record disallowed, Eldridge fitted a crude reverse mechanism and a week later set an official record at 234.93 kph (146.01 mph). This was to be the last time the record was taken on a road. In the future, sandy beaches, salt lakes and deserts were to be the venues on which specially designed and built cars fought for honours.

In between the feats of Lee Guinness and Eldridge, another Englishman, driving the same Sunbeam as Guinness, had twice broken KLG's record, each time to have the record disallowed because of arguments

over timing methods. His name was Malcolm Campbell and he was to play a major role in the history of the world land speed record.

Before that happened, however, he figured in a tragic episode at Fanoe, Denmark. The Sunbeam had been fitted with a new streamlined body built by Boulton & Paul, the aircraft manufacturers. But the beach was in poor condition and spectators crowded dangerously close. The Sunbeam was travelling at around 241.35 kph (150 mph) when it began to slew sideways – the offside front tyre had come off. Travelling at terrific speed, it hurtled into the crowd and killed a boy. Campbell managed to bring his Sunbeam to rest but the meeting was abandoned.

One good thing emerged from the fatality. The apparently guilty 'beaded-edge' and 'straight-sided' tyres (the latter were on the car when the accident happened) were put in the dock by the Dunlop Rubber Company and from their investigations emerged better and safer tyres.

Campbell next took the Sunbeam to Pendine Sands, in Wales, where, after four runs in each direction, he just managed to beat the Eldridge record by 0.24 kph (0.15 mph). The crown sat shakily on Campbell's head and well he knew it. Sunbeam were said to be building a car for Segrave; the gifted engineer, Parry Thomas, was hard at work on his own car at Brooklands; and in Paris a mysterious Italian was said to be building a car financed by an equally mysterious Egyptian prince. Campbell put in hand plans for a new car for himself, to be powered by a 450-hp Napier-Lion aero engine.

It soon became obvious that some of the contenders would be ready before Campbell. So he decided to have one more crack in the old Sunbeam, hoping that this time conditions at Pendine would be better.

The same streamlined body with discs on the rear wheels was retained, but longer exhaust pipes were fitted and the windscreen was discarded. Everything went without a hitch and at 242.75 kph (150.87 mph) Campbell became the first man to set the world record above 241 kph (150 mph), a feat which captured world imagination.

Now a truly formidable contender was unveiled. Designer Louis Coatalen's *Ladybird* was based upon his successful Sunbeam Grand Prix cars. Light and compact, it was powered by a 3,976 cc V12 engine, generally thought to be the result of two Grand Prix engines 'suitably mated', as one writer put it. To boost the comparatively small power plant a supercharger was fitted. The record bid was to be made on an 11.26 km (7 mile) stretch of sand at Southport (many years later to be the training ground of that most successful of Grand National horses, Red Rum). Coatalen hoped that the car's lightness would enable it to reach maximum speed in the limited space available. And to perfect his plans he had the outstanding British racing driver of the time, Henry Segrave. Segrave, born in the USA of an English father and American mother, had recently won both the French and Spanish Grands Prix.

With the car renamed *Tiger* all was set. . . .

Alas, the supercharger gave endless trouble and when, on Segrave's return run, the car took off for 18.3 m (60 ft) and the startled driver inadvertently rammed his foot down, the supercharger broke. When the figures were worked out, Segrave was fractionally slower than Campbell over the mile, but his kilometre time was 245.09 kph (152.33 mph), enough to make him the new record holder.

An oil-stained genius in a Fair Isle pullover was to make both Segrave and Campbell look puny. Parry

Thomas, the idol of Brooklands, had purchased the Higham Special from the estate of the late Count Zborowski. The Special was powered by a 26,907 cc V12 Liberty aero engine. Thomas lengthened the front, streamlined the tail – and lapped Brooklands at 202.73 kph (126 mph).

Thus in April 1926, Parry Thomas and *Babs*, as the Higham was now called, turned up at Pendine Sands, beat Segrave's record by 27.30 kph (16.97 mph), then went out the following day and upped it to 275.17 kph (171.02 mph). Temporarily satisfied, Parry Thomas retreated to his workshop at Brooklands to study ways and means of making *Babs* go still faster.

The following year Campbell's new *Bluebird* was ready. Mainly designed by Amherst Villiers and nearly three years in the building, it was powered by a 450-hp 12-cylinder Napier-Lion aero engine. Taken to Pendine, it sank in the sand and had to be hauled out. Gearbox, clutch and other troubles followed and on one run sea shells cut the tyres and the car skidded into marker posts. Finally, in good conditions, a perfect run gave Campbell a speed of 288 kph (179 mph). But on the return run the car hit a bump, wind, sand and water blotted out Campbell's vision and he had to hold the car on course with one hand while trying to clear his eyes and goggles with the other. Despite having to slow, his figures turned out to be 281.38 kph (174.88 mph) over the kilometre and 280.3 kph (174.2 mph) over the mile.

With Segrave en route to the States to attempt the record at Daytona, Parry Thomas and *Babs* returned to Pendine. After two very fast runs the car set off again. This time one of the ageing driving chains broke, tore through the light aluminium fairing and flailed into the cockpit, almost beheading the driver. A wheel came off, the car slide upside down for some distance, burst into flames and finally came to rest right side up, but Thomas, of course, was dead. The car was subsequently buried in Pendine Sands, but was disinterred in 1969.

Segrave's new car was more than twice the size of *Bluebird*, the record-holder. It was powered by two Matabele aero engines, one fore and one aft, giving it 44,880 cc.

Because of the potential of this giant car it was decided that Segrave would need a stretch of at least 14.5 km (9 miles) to start up, cover the measured mile and slow down again. Hence the decision to go to Daytona where there was a stretch of almost 37 km (23 miles). Tyres to withstand speeds of 321.8 kph (200 mph) were another problem. Dunlop produced some but would only guarantee their life for $3\frac{1}{2}$ minutes, just enough time to cover the measured mile and come to rest again, a frighteningly slim line of safety. When news came of the death of Parry Thomas, another check was made on the Sunbeam's driving chains, although these were already covered in armour-plate fairings.

On 29 March, 1927, Segrave smashed all previous records and became the first man in the world to beat 321.8 kph (200 mph). But not without incident. . . .

On his first run, the brakes failed. The heat had been so tremendous that the aluminium brake-shoes had melted. Segrave, faced with the choice of ploughing into 30,000 spectators, driving ahead into the river, or swerving off into the sea, chose the latter. At about 96.5 kph (60 mph) the car went into the sea in a great gust of spray. It slowed, swerved landwards and Segrave calmly drove ashore again. The mechanics fitted new brake-shoes and he made the return run, the mean time being 327.90 kph (203.79 mph), nearly 48 kph (30 mph) better than Campbell's record.

This time, however, three new cars were being built to challenge Segrave's record. For the first time since before the war, two were American.

One was a giant. Sponsored by a wealthy Philadelphia businessman, J.H. White, the White-Triplex was probably the ugliest machine ever to attempt the record. There was little or no streamlining, and the car relied entirely upon the brute force of three giant Liberty aero engines, one mounted in front of the driver and the others side by side behind him.

The Welsh wizard, J.G. Parry Thomas, in his Leyland-Thomas Special at Brooklands. An impression by Roy Nockolds.

The second, the *Black Hawk* Stutz, was a little beauty. Painted white despite its name, it had an engine of only 3,000 cc, making it one of the smallest cars ever to try for the title. It had cost £30,000, a great deal of money at the time. The White, however, had 27 times its capacity.

The third contender was, of course, Malcolm Campbell's new *Bluebird*. It had streamlined fairings in front of and behind the wheels and a tail-fin to help keep it on a straight course. The engine was a 940-hp Napier-Lion which had been developed for the victorious British aircraft in the 1927 Schneider Trophy Race.

So, in February, 1928, *Bluebird*, White-Triplex and Stutz all appeared at Daytona.

After some hazardous trial runs, Campbell beat Segrave's record with 332.99 kph (206.96 mph).

Two days later, the *Black Hawk* Stutz came out for a crack at the record. It was being driven by its main designer and builder, Frank Lockhart, winner of the 1926 Indianapolis 500 and race-leader in 1927 until a con-rod broke. The young Californian, a shrewd engineer, had also taken many international class records.

Despite wind and rain, Lockhart was soon travelling around the 321.8 kph (200 mph) mark. But a gust of wind caught the car which skidded and ran into the sea, fortunately without serious damage to either machine or man.

That left the White-Triplex. Another crack Indianapolis driver, Ray Keech, had been engaged for the attempt. But he, like Lockhart, ended up in hospital, a water connection having burst and scalded him.

Two months later, Keech, at the cost of several frights and a burned arm, registered 333.95 kph (207.55 mph). He was not around to break records for long, however, for, after winning Indianapolis in 1929, he was killed at a race meeting at Altoona.

Lockhart, too, met a grim fate. His *Black Hawk* skidded and overturned at speed. Lockhart was thrown out and killed instantly. With the deaths of him and Parry Thomas, the world of record-breaking had lost its two best driver-engineers.

Meanwhile Segrave regained the record with anti-climatic ease, registering 372.39 kph (231.44 mph). The car was the *Golden Arrow*, designed by Captain J.S. Irving, chief engineer of the Sunbeam Company.

Segrave at speed in *Golden Arrow* at Daytona Beach, USA. A painting by F. Gordon Crosby.

Beautifully streamlined, it was probably the loveliest car ever built for record attempts, the body being built by the famous carriage makers, Thrupp & Maberly, to fit the driver. Irving had borrowed Campbell's idea and the car was powered by a Schneider Trophy engine. In front of Segrave was a gun-sight so that he could, literally, aim the car. Segrave returned to England and was knighted by King George V. Campbell heard the news halfway across the world in South Africa, where he was preparing once more to attack the record.

After some hair-raising experiences at Daytona, Campbell had sought another strip and had found one at a dried-up lake-bed known as Verneuk Pan. But on his birthday, 11 March, came the news that Segrave had established a new record. It was disastrous news for Campbell since *Bluebird* had only been designed for a speed around 370 kph (230 mph) and so the attempt was doomed from the outset. He consoled himself by setting a new five-mile record at 339.50 kph (211 mph), but it was scant consolation.

The mysterious Egyptian challenger, *Djelmo*, had at last been completed, but met an inglorious end on Pendine Sands. Although the car was a write-off the Italian driver, Foresti, was thrown clear and miraculously unhurt.

Another Sunbeam challenger appeared. At 9.4 m (31 ft) long and with 4,000-hp engines, it dwarfed even the White-Triplex. Driven by the British racing motorist, Kaye Don, it was christened the *Silver Bullet*, but although from the same stable, it proved no match for *Golden Arrow* and its best speed at Daytona was a miserable 299.27 kph (186 mph).

Far away in New Zealand, 'Wizard' Smith fared little better in a Napier-Lion special, somewhat similar to the *Arrow* in looks. The similarity ended there, because although Smith got her up to more than 321 kph (200 mph) he was never in reach of Segrave's record.

Campbell rebuilt *Bluebird*, using the latest and more powerful Napier Schneider Trophy engine. He returned to Daytona in 1933 and averaged 245.74 mph over the mile and 246.09 mph over the kilometre. This time he was determined to keep the record, and Reid Railton immediately commenced work on modifications designed to make *Bluebird* even faster.

Like Segrave before him, Campbell was knighted. Returning to the States with the modified car, he became the first man to exceed 402 kph (250 mph), the official figure being 408.64 kph (253.97 mph). Again Railton got to work: the car was lengthened and strengthened and a Rolls-Royce racing aeroplane engine, fantastically light for the tremendous power it generated, was installed.

By February 1933 Campbell was back in Daytona, greeted by a brass band and with 50,000 spectators watching his attempts. He pushed the record up to 438.39 kph (272.46 mph) in spite of being handicapped by an injured left arm and a touch of influenza. For once Campbell seemed to have the field to himself; Segrave had been killed on Lake Windermere while attacking the world water speed record and none of the other contenders could get near *Bluebird*.

Just the same, it was back to the drawing-board for the *Bluebird* team. There was no need for a new engine since the Rolls-Royce had plenty in hand, but a lot of speed was being lost through wheelspin. Twin rear wheels were fitted and a new design of rear-axle, and in January 1935 Daytona saw the equipage once again.

At Verneuk Pan Cambell had found that a white line painted down the centre of the course had been a great help in keeping the car straight. He mentioned this to the Daytona authorities, and a line two feet wide was painted in lampblack and oil, a practice which became standard for record bids. *Bluebird* made a number of runs, with varying fortune, but it was not until 7 March that a serious attempt was possible.

Against the wind, *Bluebird* slightly improved upon the record, but on the return journey the car hit a bump and took off for more than 9 m (30 ft). Campbell managed to keep it under control and when the car came finally to rest the world record had been raised to 445.39 kph (276.81 mph). The team felt that the car was capable of greater things and stayed on at Daytona for another eight weeks, hoping for an improvement in the conditions. The improvement never came.

Over the years an American Mormon, Ab Jenkins, had set a tremendous number of long-distance records in his car, the *Mormon Meteor*, on the salt flats at Bonneville, Utah.

The Campbell team repaired there and, after an exciting series of incidents which included the car catching fire, Campbell raised the record to 484.52 kph (301.13 mph). Like Segrave before him, he decided that it was time to turn his attention to the water speed record. He had broken the land speed record no less than nine times and had been personally responsible for adding 112.6 kph (70 mph) to it.

Other British drivers were only too ready to pick up the torch. An eminent engineer-driver, Captain George Eyston, who already had a bagful of small car records to his name, now appeared in a giant called the *Thunderbolt* which weighed nearly seven tons, and took the record at 502 kph (312 mph). From then until the outbreak of the Second World War, the record was to be a shuttlecock between Eyston and a fellow-countryman, John Cobb. Eyston pushed the figure up to 555.11 kph (345 mph), Cobb in his much lighter Napier-Railton travelled at 563.15 kph (350 mph), Eyston did 574.41 kph (357 mph). Finally, in 1939, with the war clouds near and ominous, Cobb returned to Utah and regained the record with 634.20 kph (394.16 mph).

The whole concept of record-breaking changed after the Second World War. Jet propulsion emerged as the new motive power for record-attempting cars, although the period began conventionally enough with normal 'drive to the wheel' cars attacking and holding the records.

Soon after peace came, 'the fastest man on earth', John Cobb, took the Napier-Railton back to the salt flats at Bonneville. On 15 September, 1947, he became the first man to travel at more than 644 kph (400 mph), clocking 648.64 kph (403.135 mph) in one direction

and averaging 634.26 kph (394.196 mph). The next day, the salt flats were flooded.

Cobb, like Segrave and Campbell, turned to the water speed record and, alas, like Segrave, he died when his craft exploded at speed.

Cobb's land record remained unchallenged for many years. However, in 1960, Donald Campbell, who had succeeded his father, Malcolm, Segrave and others in becoming the world water speed king, brought out a new *Bluebird* to attempt the land speed record. But when he arrived in Utah he found three

American teams on the spot, all ready to have a crack at Cobb's record. Another American, Athol Graham, had been killed trying to break the record earlier that summer.

Mickey Thompson, who was still breaking records a decade later, was the most serious of the American challengers. In a car powered by four supercharged Pontiac engines he did, in fact, clock a record-breaking 653.23 kph (406 mph) in one direction, but had trouble on the return run and retired from the fray to work on his car and come back another time.

Campbell, meanwhile, had been undergoing trials in which he reported that the car was handling well but the course was tricky. After a run at more than 482.7 kph (300 mph), Campbell decided to try an acceleration test. Travelling at something like 587 kph (365 mph), the car took off and bounced four times before coming to a halt facing the direction from which it had come.

The 1961 version of *Bluebird*, the name given to the record-breakers on land and water, of father and son, Sir Malcolm and Donald Campbell.

Campbell, recovering in hospital, announced that as soon as car and driver were ready, he would have another go. Sir Alfred Owen, whose firm had built the car, said that if the driver had the guts to try again, Owens would rebuild the car.

The car was worth rebuilding. It was the first car designed for the land speed record to have a gas turbine engine, the Bristol Siddeley Proteus 755 turbo-prop, or, in engineering terms, a free turbine. It drove all four wheels of *Bluebird* and although no one knew it at the time, it was to be one of the last two cars to hold the record and have direct drive from engine to wheels. Soon the record was to be taken by the true jets, without direct drive and relying on their tremendous power for propulsion.

But, for the present, *Bluebird* held the stage. The engine was of the same type as that used to propel the fastest warships of the time, the Royal Navy's 'Brave' class patrol boats. It delivered high power for its bulk and weight. At full throttle the engine would develop 4,250 hp, the equivalent of a top speed of around 804.5 kph (500 mph). Yet it was only 1.01 m (40 in) in diameter, just over 2.4 m (8 ft) long and weighed about 1,361 kg (3,000 lb). It required no cooling system and no clutch because it used the equivalent of a fluid torque converter, the output shaft being coupled

directly and permanently to bevel gears in the front and rear axles. The turbine provided no engine braking on the overrun at low speeds, but at 644 kph (400 mph) about 500 hp would be available for braking if the throttle were closed. In fact, two braking systems provided the stopping power: air flaps opening out from the rear of the car and power-operated Girling disc brakes on all four wheels.

The overall weight of the car was four tons. It measured 9.14 m (30 ft) long, 2.4 m (8 ft) wide and 1.45 m (4 ft 9 in) high without its removable tail fin. It ran on aviation turbine kerosene – and at full speed *Bluebird* did $1\frac{1}{2}$ miles to the gallon. There was one other point of interest – the tyres, 132.1 cm (52 in) in diameter, were the largest ever made for a land vehicle at that time.

It was the most expensive and advanced car ever built when Donald Campbell took it to Lake Eyre in South Australia in March, 1963. The result was miserable and frustrating. No rain had fallen at Lake Eyre for seven years – but now it rained. And rained.

In 1964, Campbell returned to Australia and answered his critics in the best fashion possible,

One of the ugliest record-breakers ever: Art Arfons' *Green Monster.*

beating Cobb's record by 14.48 kph (9 mph). Campbell's speed over the mile in both directions was identical – 648.59 kph (403.1 mph). He was disappointed, however, that he had failed to go faster than the 655.59 kph (407.45 mph) of American Craig Breedlove's *Spirit of the Age*. Breedlove's three-wheeler was technically a motor-cycle, but Campbell was right to see in this jet-propelled vehicle from America the shape of things to come.

In October, 1964, Tom Green, driving the jet *Wingfoot Express*, clocked 664.8 kph (413.2 mph) and Art Arfons in the *Green Monster* followed this up with 698.63 kph (434.2 mph).

The jet-age had come. . . .

In December, the FIA, representing cars, and the FIM, motor-cycles, got together to clear up the confusion caused by the appearance of jets and three-wheelers on the record scene. Jointly, they laid down new definitions for the land speed record.

For the first time, an official land speed record was recognized by both FIA and FIM. It was open to any vehicle which depended upon the ground for its support during its record run and which was steered by a driver in the vehicle who could also control acceleration and deceleration. Four-wheel attempts would be controlled by the FIA and three- or two-wheel attempts by the FIM. The best performance by a *normal* automobile or motor-cycle, irrespective of class, would be known as world records.

Thus 1965 dawned with the situation clear. There were two records to be broken, Donald Campbell's 648.43 kph (403 mph) in a normal automobile and Art Arfon's 862.42 kph (536 mph) in a jet with power not transmitted directly to the wheels.

A fantastic assortment of cars were to appear at Bonneville to challenge these figures.

Only one was a normal automobile, if such a term can be applied to a record-breaker. Designed and built by brothers Bill and Bob Summers, from Los Angeles, one a machinist, the other a truck driver, the Chrysler-engined *Goldenrod* was a low-slung beauty which rivalled Segrave's *Golden Arrow* as the most attractive record-breaker ever. Shaped like a needle and 9.75 m (32 ft) long, *Goldenrod* broke Campbell's record on 12 November, with a speed of 658.08 kph (409 mph). It was a pity for the Summers brothers that their valiant effort was overshadowed by the activity of the faster jet set.

While Donald Campbell's long-drawn-out attack on the conventional record had been going on, the jets had been busy. Walter Arfons, half-brother of Art, with his drivers Tom Green and Bob Patroe, had clocked 664.5 kph (413 mph) in the *Wingfoot Express*; Art beat this figure comfortably three days later; and then Craig Breedlove, in his three-wheeled *Spirit of America* registered first 754.17 kph (468.72 mph) and then 846.78 kph (526.28 mph) in the course of which

he wrecked his vehicle. The *Green Monster* reached 863.57 kph (536.71 mph), but was also somewhat the worse for wear afterwards.

Breedlove set the 1965 season rolling when, on 2 November, in his new *Spirit of America*, he beat Art Arfons' time by almost 30.57 kph (19 mph). The car was a beautifully streamlined machine looking very much like the fuselage of an aircraft, complete to pointed nose and tail-plane. It was now an automobile and not a motor-cycle, the original three-wheel layout having been replaced by four. The J79 engine exerted a thrust of 15,000 pounds and so, as with most of the jet record cars, a parachute was needed to assist the normal braking system in slowing the car down. In this car, Breedlove set a record of 893.77 kph (555.483 mph).

Five days later the *Green Monster*, likened by the press to 'a garbage truck', clocked 927.67 kph (576.55 mph).

Breedlove was far from finished. Despite rain which left puddles on one end of the course, he averaged 966.51 kph (600.69 mph), the first man to set the record at over 965 kph (600 mph).

Appropriately enough it was a frustrated astronaut who carved another niche in record-breaking history. Gary Gabelich dropped out of the space programme when he found he was not going to be able to pilot the spaceship. Instead he raced dragsters, motor-cycles and powerboats. By 1968, he held the world water speed record for dragboats, thus following very much in the steps of Segrave, Cobb and the Campbells. And so in 1970, the 30-year-old Gabelich, with the hippy haircut and mannerisms, arrived at the salt flats with *Blue Flame*.

Blue Flame, in the words of its driver, 'is basically a long piece of pipe, 38.2 feet from nose to tail, 8.8 feet to the top of its tailfin, 7.8 feet wide, and weighing 6,500 pounds'. The rocket engine (770 pounds) was designed to produce 16,000 pounds of thrust, the equivalent of 58,000 horsepower. And the car could accelerate from 0–650 mph in 20 seconds. Finished off in silver and blue, *Blue Flame* looked every inch a formidable contender.

So it proved. . . .

After some 20 runs during which he was frequently close to the record, Gabelich registered 1,001.45 kph (622.407 mph), his fastest run being over 1,013.7 kph (630 mph) for the kilometre.

Eight years have passed and still Gabelich holds the record. Will it be beaten? Gabelich himself has plans for a 1,000 mph car. In England, Project Thrust is hoping to build a car for a man named Richard Noble to drive; and the Campbells' chief backroom boy, Leo Villa, is working on another project.

But the Bonneville Salt Flats are breaking up. It is doubtful if anyone now will ever travel faster than Gabelich on the dried-up lake beds of Utah, USA.

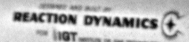

In contrast to the *Green Monster*, the elegant torpedo-shaped *Blue Flame* in which Gary Gabelich took the world land speed record.

Index

Page numbers in italics refer to illustration captions

Acknowledgements

The publishers would like to thank the following individuals and organizations for their kind permission to reproduce the photographs in this book. They would also like to thank owners who kindly allowed their cars to be photographed.

The Bettman Archive 8, 39 above, 88 below; Custom Car Magazine 89; Daily Telegraph Colour Library Front and Back Jacket; Daimler-Benz 6; Mary Evans Picture Library 9, 11, 24 above, 24 below, 27, 35 above inset, 37 above, 41; Angelo Hornak 30; Louis Klemantaski 64 inset, 67 inset right, 70 above centre, 70 below centre, 70 below, 78 centre, 78 below, 79; Mansell Collection 20–21; Pete Myers 10, 12 above, 12 centre, 12 below, 13 above, 14, 16, 23 below inset, 25, 43 above; The National Motor Museum 98–99, 100; Cyril Posthumus 102–103; Peter Roberts 22, 28–29, 35, 57 above inset, 57 below inset, 60, 61, 64, 67 inset left, 69 below, 74, 80 below, 81, 88 above; Royal Automobile Club (Pete Myers) 62–63, 76–77, 93, 94–95; Spectrum Colour Library 37 below; Jasper Spencer-Smith 23 above, 43 below, 44 left, 49, 50–51, 87 inset; Tony Stone Associates Ltd. 19, 42, 46, 65, 65 inset, 67, 71, 75, 78 above; Syndication International 32–33, 79 above inset, 79 below inset, 80 above, 90, 96–97; Nicky Wright Endpapers, 13 below, (Owner: L.B. Goldsmith) 15, (Owner: Roy Middleton) 17, (Owner: Bob Hughes, "Yesterdays Wheels") 18, 44 right, 45 inset, 45, 46 above inset, 46 below inset, 47, 48, 49 inset left, 49 inset right, (Owner: J. Gordon) 51 inset, 52 above, 52 below, 54 left, 54 right, 55, 56–57, 59, 66, 70 above, 72 above left, 72 above right, 72 centre, 72 below left, 72 below right, (Owner: Stroud Motors) 82, 83, (Owner: M.J. Sherman) 84 above, 84 below inset, (Owner: S. Lawton) 85, (Owner: S. Lawton) 85 inset, 86–87.

Picture Research by Thelma Gilbert.

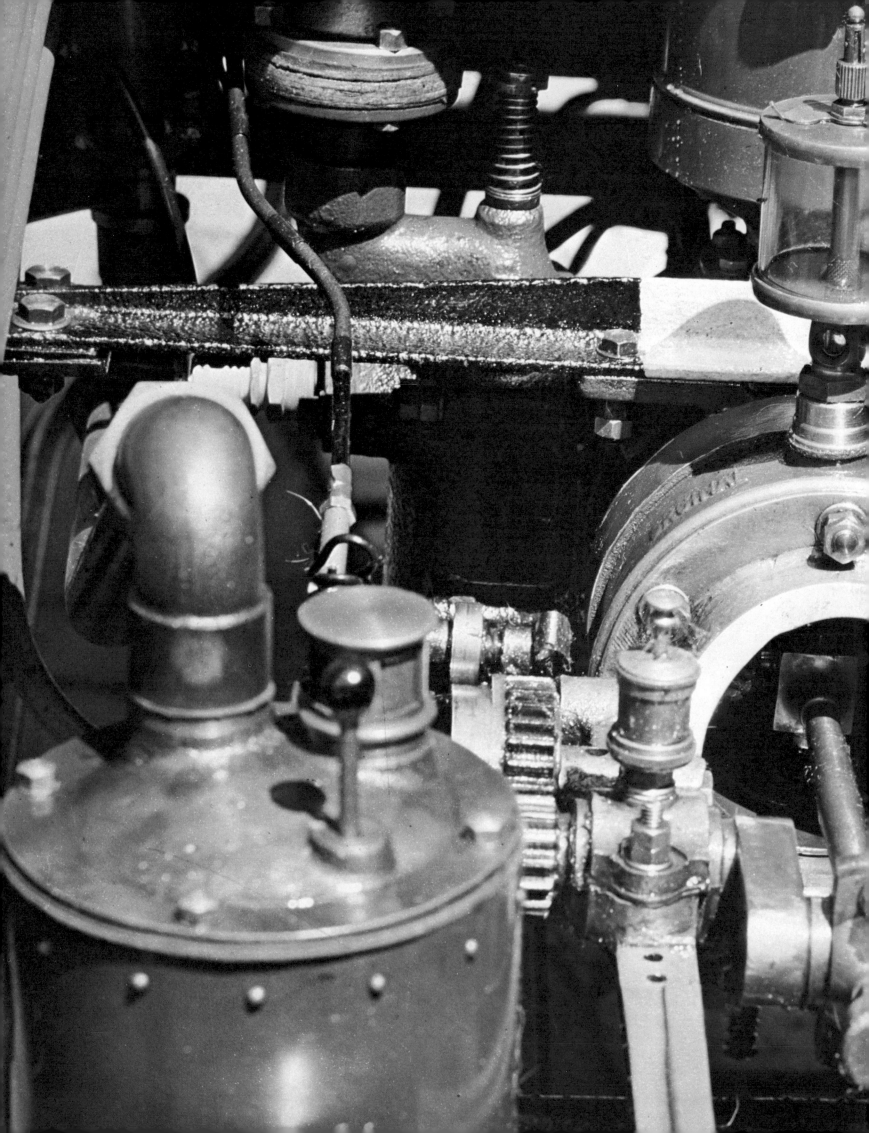